AF480113

Reflections on My Humble Beginnings

By Pema Tango

Contents

Dedication

Inside the pages of this book, I have attempted to capture my life's journey, the challenges I faced, and the triumphs I experienced. More than anything, it is a celebration of the relationships that have shaped me into the person I am today. Without the love and support of cherished daughter, Zoya Zumsel Thinley, and my dear parents, Richard Meade and Kenneth Bavaria (known fondly as Daddy and Grandpa in this book), I truly believe that this endeavor would not have been possible.

Zoya, you are the light of my life. Your unwavering belief in me, even during the most difficult times, has been a constant source of inspiration. You have shown me strength and resilience, and it is an honor to have you by my side as I dedicate this book to you. May it serve as a reminder of the love we share and dreams we inspire to achieve.

Daddy and Grandpa, you have been my pillars of support from the very beginning. Your decision to adopt me and provide me with loving home transformed my life in unimaginable ways. Not only did you give me a chance to receive an education, but you also invested your time and effort into tutoring me. Your belief in my abilities pushed me to persevere, and your guidance has shaped me into the person I am today. This book is a testament to your unyielding love, and I am eternally grateful.

Thank you for being the guiding lights in my life. Your love encouragement, and support have given me the strength to pursue my dreams, and this special dedication, with the world.

Acknowledgements

Additionally I want to acknowledge my Alaskan parents Steven and Suzanne Malter Parker and family, who initially brought me to this country, USA.

Chapter 1: Reflections

There is a story that should prove quite entertaining to read and captures some revealing reasons for an East Asian to totally uproot his existence for a chance at success in the greatest country in the world - America. I essentially altered my orientation from Buddhist monk to hopeful acclimation to a totally different environment, which would allow me to express my lifelong yearnings. Please allow me the indulgence to share a little about my upbringing and the meaningful experiences that shaped me into the person I am today.

I was born in the mid-1970s in Ney Pema Choeling, a small village in Kurtoey Lhuntse, Bhutan. My parents, Phurpa la and Ngoshang were hardworking farmers who did their best to provide for our family of seven, including myself and my four siblings. Although they never had the opportunity to attend school and get a good education themselves, they always encouraged us to pursue it, knowing it was our path to a prosperous life.

During my parents' childhood years, school was seen as a form of punishment rather than a gateway to knowledge. Their parents would shed tears when their children were chosen to attend school. Despite their circumstances, my parents were self-taught individuals and possessed a rare practical wisdom that made them revered pillars in our village. My father, in particular, was christened "Uncle" to the whole community and was always ready to lend a helping hand to those in need.

One memorable incident that encapsulated the fortitude of my father was when he encountered a black bear one morning while tending to our livestock. With sheer strength and courage, he managed to overpower the bear, albeit losing his pinky toe in the process. Months later, when the bear was killed, the villagers recognized it as the same bear my father had fought, as it bore the scars of the encounter. It was a testament to my father's strength and resilience, and yet, throughout his life, he remained a gentle soul.

Growing up, my family led a simple life, unaware of economic hardships. In my eyes, my parents always had enough rice to sustain us, and that was enough. For us, being able to produce our food made us feel rich. An example of our humble existence was not until the age of nine, when I joined the monastery that I wore shoes for the first time.

At the age of six, I began assisting my father in herding our cows. Together, we would journey to different places, often finding shelter in caves next to warm fires, with calves nearby. There was a certain charm to those moments. I recall sleeping between my parents, refusing to separate for the evening. Their nightly and morning prayers became comforting, and I soon memorized the prayers, joining with them as one devoted unit. During these childhood moments, I found solace and fostered a sense of spirituality. As I grew older, I gradually took on the responsibility of cow herding independently, demonstrating a level of maturity uncommon for someone of my age. The villagers viewed me as an exemplary young leader, inspiring others to fulfill their destinies.

Although my father was uneducated, his foresight was remarkable. One aspect of my childhood was that at a young age, my father recognized my potential and arranged for me to learn basic reading and writing skills from my cousin, who had some formal education. I would eagerly wake up early in the morning and spend a couple of hours each day learning with my cousin. Thanks to his guidance, I almost completed the required subjects necessary for a monk's "nursery school" education (the beginning aspect of monkhood). These early experiences instilled in me a deep appreciation for education and ignited a thirst for knowledge that continues to drive me to this day.

I was always eager to lend a hand to my hardworking parents. One sunny day, I decided to venture into the nearby jungle in search of fiddleheads, a vegetable that my family loved to collect. Determined to prove my bravery and assert my childish masculinity, I set off on my adventure with my loyal companion, Lajan La, a playful and protective dog. I had been to this part of the jungle before and had accompanied my father a few times to gather bamboo, so I felt confident in navigating the area. As I ventured further into the dense vegetation, excitement mingled with a slight sense of insecurity. Engrossed in my task, I suddenly heard a rustling noise from a nearby thicket of trees. In an instant, my Lajan La's ears perked up, and he let out a worried squeal. At first, he was ahead of me, being that the tradition of dog ownership in Bhutan did not require leashing our pets. Turning to see what caused that alarm, my heart skipped a beat. There, munching on hazelnuts, stood a black bear!

Panicking, I quickly gathered the harvested fiddleheads and sprinted away as fast as my little legs could carry me. Sometimes, the dog took the lead, and in other moments, I would lead, but always Lajan La would be aware of my safety. To this day, I am plagued by the idea of if I was in danger, would he come to my rescue and how would he respond if the bear accosted me?" or would the bear prey upon either of us. We did manage to run and run, with the bear's growls echoing behind us, and eventually, we reached the safety of Goenpa, a place of peace and refuge high in the hills a little further in elevation than the village, where Lopen Tsampa Ngawang Phuntso's family lived.

With tear-filled eyes and trembling lips, I recounted my terrifying encounter to Ani Thinley Palden, Tsampa's wife, who listened attentively. Ani comforted me, assuring me I was safe now and need not worry anymore. Her gentle demeanor and soothing words eased my fear, bringing a sense of relief to this young farmer child. While my heart slowly stopped racing, Ani gave me valuable advice. She advised me not to venture deep into the jungle alone in the future, emphasizing the importance of this lesson.

With a mixture of relief and amusement, Ani relayed the story of my encounter to my parents. She couldn't help but chuckle as she spoke of how pitifully scared I was, and yet, in all the chaos, I had clung onto the fiddleheads collected before the incident. My parents were thankful for Ani's care and comfort, but they couldn't help but laugh at the comical image of their brave little farmer child clutching vegetables amidst danger. They marveled at my determination, knowing I had learned a valuable lesson that day about bravery, responsibility, and the importance of not leaving tasks unfinished. From that day forward, I continued to help my parents on the farm, always mindful of my safety. I had learned lessons in the jungle, and although my adventures became more mundane, my bravery and sense of responsibility never wavered as I grew into a wise and earnest young child.

Our village was quite remote, and traveling to the nearest city seemed like a journey to another world. It took a whole day on foot to reach the city, and my parents occasionally made the trip for shopping. Our village was believed to be Guru Rinpoche's sacred place, and as children, we would play in the rice fields, pretending to be hunters or archers. I had a particular aversion to harming birds and would often fight with others to save them. This compassion earned me praise from my father, who was proud of my kindness.

One memory that still stays vivid in my mind was when I was around six years old, and my family and I embarked on a unique adventure to a hot spring located high up in the mountains during the winter season. This hot spring was known for its healing properties and was considered a luxury vacation for farmers like us.

The journey to the hot spring was far from easy. It took us approximately five hours to reach the destination by foot, navigating through a narrow, often barely visible path. However, despite the difficulty, we were determined to enjoy this retreat. We pitched our tent-like hut and collected wood for cooking, making ourselves home in this rugged yet captivating place. One thing that stood out about this location was the stories we heard of a mystical presence called Yeti, otherwise known as Big Foot. The locals would often share tales about encountering strange occurrences in this area involving Yeti, adding an air of mystery to our adventure. The hot spring was below a towering cliff, with a breathtaking waterfall cascading downward. The cliff was adorned with sacred symbols and religious imagery, further emphasizing the sanctity of this place. These images fascinated us, and we would spend hours exploring the area and immersing ourselves in the healing water.

Each morning, around 4:30 AM, I would wake up to the sounds of cows mooing, roosters crowing, and the distant echoes of religious instruments being played. As a child, I assumed these sounds were coming from beyond the mountain, possibly from a Tibetan village far across Bhutan's border. Excitedly, I would wake my father, excited it was time to start our day because the roosters were singing and the monks were chanting. The roosters' piercing singing acted as our traditional alarm clock. However, to my surprise, my father couldn't hear the sounds I was referring to. I was becoming agitated that no one else could hear the sounds. He peppered me with questions, and confused, he discussed this with other individuals in the morning, who speculated that these sounds were somehow coming through the shrouded mystery of the heavenly sacred place that sparked our imagination.

Another incident that left a lasting impression on me was one night during our excursion; we were having dinner in the hut by the fire. Suddenly, we heard a human voice from afar, originating from the other side of the mountain. Startled, my sister and I instinctively jumped into the nearest corner of the hut, seeking comfort from our family. Trying to calm our fears, my father suggested that it might have been a group of mountaineers passing by. However, he later shared with others that it was believed to be the presence of the legendary Yeti. To this day, the Bhutanese government carries on an active investigation into the whereabouts of the Yeti and any other mysterious life forms in that particular region. On a sadder note, my father's brother had traversed the mountain where the Yeti sightings were accounted for. He returned to our village, recounting this eventful trip and trembling with fear because of the Yeti sighting. This was too powerful an image for his mind to process, and he passed away that morning. We believe it was because of the purported supernatural imagery. These memories from that trip have stayed with me over the years, bringing me joy and sadness and serving as a reminder of the wonders and mysteries that this world holds. It was an adventure filled with both beauty and intrigue, and I am grateful to have experienced it with my family and relatives from the village.

I must confess, though, that I was not always a well-behaved child. One incident that still brings shame upon me is when I mischievously peed on my sister's and her friend's heads while perched high up in a tree, claiming it as my territory. It was an act of rebellion that I deeply regret to this day. In the countryside, it was customary for children to drink local alcohol from a young age. I indulged in this practice and found it to be part of the norm during my early years, nevertheless not abusing this coveted privilege.

One particular aspect that set me apart was others' belief that I was the reincarnation of a holy man from Tibet. During my mother's pregnancy, a holy man renowned for his meditation and predictions approached both my parents. He revealed that I was believed to be the reincarnation of a holy man from Tibet. At the moment of my birth, this revelation was finally verified by a physical sign – an unusual curl of hair in the center of my head. This was similar to the hairstyle of a meditator, indicating profound spiritual achievements and bestowed an immense sense of wonder and joy upon both my parents.

As I began to speak, my words and mannerisms were peculiar. I spoke of past stories reminiscent of an old wise man and requested to be taken to places unknown to my family. These incidents only deepened the belief that there was something extraordinary about my being. At the age of four, an onset of muteness took hold of me, rendering me unable to speak for six months. In despair, my parents invited a layman to perform a ritual, and miraculously, in the middle of that very night, my speech returned – a moment that filled both my parents with awe and gratitude. Since then, the ritual has become a vital part of our lives, with my parents and my sisters continuing to perform it periodically on my behalf. During my period of muteness, I vividly recall an unpleasant memory. One day, as I was walking home from the cornfield where my father was working, I came across a fruit that resembled corn and looked ripe and delicious. In my mother tongue, it is called "Jagpa," little did I know that it was highly poisonous.

Out of curiosity, I plucked two or three seeds from the fruit and ate them. Almost immediately, the poison took effect, and I started drooling excessively. As I stumbled towards my mother, she noticed something was terribly wrong and began to panic. Desperate for answers, she asked me what had happened, but I could only communicate through gestures and facial expressions.

Realizing that something was seriously wrong, I guided her towards the tree where I found the fruit, dragging her towards it. When she saw the fruit, she instantly knew what had transpired. It was as if her years of wisdom and ancestral knowledge kicked in, allowing her to act swiftly. My mother quickly made a decision and instructed me to urinate, allowing me to drink my own urine. Although it may sound unusual, this was an indigenous medicine practiced during those times, as they had limited access to hospitals and modern healthcare. Incredibly, this unconventional remedy had a curative effect on my condition.

As reflected in that moment of my personal history, I am amazed by the ingenuity and survival techniques that people in that region possessed. They were incredibly resourceful, utilizing whatever means they had to protect and heal their loved ones. In the absence of modern medical facilities, their knowledge and reliance on traditional practices saved countless lives.

Had my mother not known what to do at that critical moment, I would have succumbed to the poison right in front of her helpless gaze. All she could have done would be to cry out load and watch her son's life fade away. This memory serves as a testament to the strength, resilience, and love that existed within our community, and it reminds me of the value of preserving and passing down that ancient wisdom to future generations.

You may be interested in the phase of my life that ended my virginity, and if not, I will tell you anyway. There is an ancient tradition in the east of Bhutan that resembles the wild days of 1960s America in terms of sexual freedom. The tradition is called "night hunting," which is the act of the boys sneaking from house to house, entering the windows of the rooms where the girls awaited, and hoping for a surreptitious romantic encounter. Of course, the fathers disapproved of such actions and would come after us with primitive lighted torches made of kindling, attempting to chase us away and preserve their daughters' dignity. My initiation into the practice involved a very humorous anecdote, which I will now reveal. I was the youngest of a randy trio, and we snuck into an unsuspecting girl's room. At that moment, her father appeared and interrupted us after preparing in the next room to extinguish our youthful hopes. He chased, and we had no other choice but to jump out the nearest window. To our despair, we landed on the cows, and the poor creatures bellowed with surprise, but we escaped except for one unfortunate soul left behind, who had twisted his ankle and had to cower painfully behind one of the cows, hoping not to be seen. Escaping detection, we waited for the father to leave and then returned to retrieve our helpless comrade. This tradition was confined to the eastern part of Bhutan. Consequently, the Westerners were fascinated by it and when traveling to the neck of the woods started participating in our antics. Need I say that from a sociological standpoint, many illegitimate births, called Kokti, were registered nine months later. This was a turning point for me, and I matured into a little trickster, conspiring to create my own immature den of inequity so that the fun could progress. My friends and I pretended to construct a childhood home partitioned by hay and built by the sweat of our brows and then invited the girls to enter our structure. They were fascinated by the proposition and moved into our simple traps. Then we would proceed to imitate night hunting, learned from the older village boys, and all of us would delight in childish fantasies. One time, I was hanging out with friends and cowherding while my father was busy at work in an adjacent field. He inadvertently wandered by and witnessed our shenanigans but pretended not to notice, turned away, and continued with his work. The next day, while talking to the other adult villagers, he shared the story while beaming proudly for his maturing son. At that moment, he was a proud papa, just as he was when I was born eight years earlier. It may not appeal to modern temperaments, but at the time, we created our own fun however we could with limited resources and an abundance of preteen hormones.

One incident at the age of eight demonstrated a streak of mischievousness which permeated my youth. My sister and I fought pretty often, and unfortunately, one time, it caused a cut to her face, which understandably upset my father very much. He was never prone to corporal punishment, but this time was too much for him to ignore, and he pummeled me with a stick, which shocked me tremendously. My immature emotions got the better of me, and I ran away into the forest to hide and cool my heels. While brooding, I decided to travel three hours by foot over the mountain to a hermit site, Goenpa, which housed spiritual devotees. Luckily, there was a family friend, Tsampa, who and his family welcomed me, accepting me with open arms, and took me on as an acolyte. The surprises didn't stop as I encountered an older neighbor boy from my village, and we renewed an earlier friendship and continued together as students. The following day, I had my first reading class, a continuation of rudimentary learning in my younger days, which proved to be beneficial to my situation. We traveled with tsampa from village to village, giving prayers and blessings in return for alms. On the way between villages, we came upon a bridge straddling the main river Kurichu, which was a dangerous passage because of the forcefulness of the water. I had no experience navigating such a narrow and long bridge. Not even my arms could reach from one side to the other. The bridge was projecting an optical illusion since I couldn't discern the movement, vertigo set in, and I almost jumped from confusion. Later, when I reached home and related this story to my parents, my dad almost had a heart attack because he was well aware of the bridge's reputation causing people to jump or fall. He explained the reality of the dangerous rushing water leading to many innocent deaths.

My friend and I were tasked with the responsibility of carrying the heavy sack of accumulated alms back to tsampa, my little back carrying the same weight as my compatriot, even though he was much bigger and older. Half way back during the darkening evening, he decided to take shelter in a village called Lingabi in a household he knew, an hour's walk to my sister's village called Tsoling. While my friend and I were resting with our sacks, Tsampa walked ahead and left us behind, thwarting the original plan of going to my sister's house. This angered me, and I told my friend I was taking a bathroom break and instead ran into the forest, with my friend noticing my intentional exit. The forest was inky black, home to wild animals such as bears, and with no discernible light, hence forcing me to rely on memory to reach my destination. When I reached my sister's house, she cried and embraced me with great emotion. I told her the circumstances of the last six horrible days, and she boiled with rage and vowed to confront him with righteous anger.

The next day, my sister instructed her husband to accompany me on the trek between her village and mine, which was an even more dangerous trip, full of dense forest, several unreliable bridges, and many stories of wild bear attacks, including my brother in law walking me being attacked resulting in horrendous damage to his face.

Chapter 2: The Acolyte

At the tender age of nine, I bid farewell to my parents, joining a monastery that would begin my journey as a monk. It was an emotional separation, but with time, I grew accustomed to my new surroundings. I was fortunate to bond with a very compassionate man who was second in line at the monastery known as Umzey Karmala. He protected me, not allowing any of the older monks in charge to abuse or chastise me. This was important to my psychic development because discipline was brutal and often meted out for the slightest infraction. Later, when at Tango University, I was able to assist him and offer him comfort during his three-year meditation programs. At this point, he treated me as an equal and was deeply impressed with my education and various accomplishments.

Near the monastery, my aunt and uncle owned a grocery store, which was very convenient and comforting to me because I would frequently visit them and bask in my aunt's kindness. She supplemented my diet by providing nutritious food, but what was even more important was that she would launder my robes and cater to my hygiene. One particular memory that remains with me is when I became infested with scabies. She would place me in the sink and make sure that all of my body, including the nether regions, was disinfected with soap and hot water. My aunt and uncle always welcomed me with open arms and were exceedingly friendly to all my relatives, especially my dearly departed father, their uncle.

Within a couple of years in the monk nursery, I excelled in the required subjects and was therefore chosen to attend a prestigious Buddhist institute, Ngatshang Shedra, which consisted of three different monasteries in the eastern sector of Bhutan, Lhuntse, Mongar, and Tashigang. There were ten monks from each of the monasteries, and we were each chosen for these coveted positions based on excelling in our requirements. I was one of the youngest monks but was regarded as the toughest, both physically and mentally. My reputation did not prevent me from forming close relationships and friendships with many of my fellow acolytes. To survive on a daily basis, we monks depended on receiving a stipend from an administrative center in Thimphu. Often, the stipends were late because of the remoteness of our center, and we would have to fend for ourselves by gathering fiddlehead ferns and mushrooms in the forest during our short lunch break. We were required to study late into the night, and to accomplish this, we needed kerosene for our lamps, which we obtained by once a month hitchhiking to Mongar for fuel. This was a tenuous situation because there were very few vehicles going through our neighborhood, but when we heard an approaching truck or car, we ran to the road in anticipation of a ride.

While living at Ngatshang Shedra, my friend and I discovered a shop nearby that had puppies for sale, and we each bought one puppy for companionship, paying one hundred ngultrum (Bhutanese currency) apiece. We brought the puppies home and enjoyed playing with them. One week later, during lunch break, I took the puppy out to feed it cow milk, and as the puppy was thoroughly enjoying drinking, I went back in to procure more milk. When I came out, a horrible action happened. A bald eagle swooped down to earth and grasped the puppy with its claws. I almost was able to grab the leash, but to no avail. In desperation, I ran into the jungle to chase the captor of my puppy but was not able to interfere with Mother Nature's tooth and claw. This incident affected me deeply, and consequently, I cried for many days.

I was not only one of the youngest students in my class but also the favorite of all my teachers. My intelligence and dedication to my studies were remarkable, earning me endless praise from my Khenpos (abbots) and teachers. Amongst all my teachers, Khenpo, the head abbot of the institute Karma Tshering, held a particular fondness for me. Khenpo Karma was head of the institute and was one of the renowned young abbots. He recognized my potential and saw something special in me. Impressed by my abilities, he made an extraordinary decision to invite me to stay with him in his room.

Excited and honored, I accepted the offer and became Khenpo's roommate. My living arrangement was different from that of other students, as I no longer had to adhere to the daily routines such as morning and evening prayers. Instead, Khenpo Karma and I spent our time together, exploring the beauty of nature that surrounded our Institute. During our walks along the road and through the enchanting forests, Khenpo Karma and I would collect mushrooms and fiddleheads. As we strolled amidst the tall trees and listened to the sounds of nature, I cherished every moment spent with my new friend and mentor. My friends couldn't help but envy my unique situation. While they were engaged in prayers and daily routines, I had the privilege of experiencing a different kind of education - one that taught me the wonders of the world outside the classroom. My friendship with Khenpo Karma brought an understanding of life that went beyond the textbooks.

However, as time passed, I started noticing a peculiar aspect of Khenpo Karma's stories. The Khenpo would often reminisce about his time studying in India, and during holiday weekends, he would share his tales of encountering beautiful women wearing bikinis along the beaches there. These stories intrigued me, and I began to recognize a longing in Khenpo Karma's voice. Curious, I contemplated the possibility that Khenpo Karma had a desire to be with these enchanting women he spoke of. My suspicions were confirmed when, after he resigned from his position and returned to Thimphu, I learned of Khenpo Karma's marriage.

Reflecting on this revelation, I understood that even though Khenpo Karma had found ultimate peace and friendship in his life, there was a part of him that longed for something different. I realized that every person has their own desires and dreams, and it was essential to respect and acknowledge them. As I studied and pursued my own dream, I reflected on the lessons learned from Khenpo Karma. Our friendship taught me not only the importance of knowledge but also the value of understanding and accepting others without judgment. I carried the wisdom of my beloved teacher with me, cherishing the memories of our walks and conversations. I would forever be grateful, knowing that being the favorite of my teachers had not only brought me recognition but also valuable lessons that would shape my journey ahead.

There was intense studying at Ngatshang, but we were relatively isolated from the central monastic body, and we had little connection with the national education council. An announcement of the schedule for exams was not forthcoming; therefore, we had no recourse but to study rigorously and await some nebulous determination from afar. Eventually, during my third year, we were given tests, and I achieved top grades, thus receiving a prize in the form of textbooks and clothing. Earning this honor built my confidence and sparked my desire to continue my academic career, and from there, I moved on to another institute in Thimphu called Dodedrak Shedra.

The journey to Dodedrak marked a significant turning point in my life. I embarked on a solo trek through the mountains, carrying a large wooden suitcase, a substantial mattress, and blankets. Despite exhaustion and hunger, I persevered while shedding tears along the way. Eventually, the sound of chatter and laughter from fellow monks on their lunch break greeted me and lifted my spirits. Introduced as a new student, I received warmth and camaraderie that reassured me in this unfamiliar place.

In due course, I was assigned a room with a roommate, and my classes began. It didn't take long for me to rise to the top of the class, impressing all the teachers and peers with my dedication and intelligence. In my second year, I was bestowed the honor of being a captain, equivalent to a teacher, bearing the requisite responsibilities with ease. While in Thimphu, I became interested in developing my physical prowess to accompany my spiritual development at school. This led me to take Tae Kwon Do classes and other physical activities. This was a forbidden activity, as we were supposed to only develop our minds while attending the monastery. I strongly disagreed with this proposition, as I have always believed the two aspects of a person, physical and spiritual, are not mutually exclusive. Other monks would accompany me and were amazed at my Tae Kwon Do abilities, which I demonstrated to their utter delight. Some became so enthralled with it that they would practice along with me, which broadened their capabilities and sense of physical accomplishment. At that tender age, we were all thrilled to build our strengths and have fun in the process.

At this time, the World Cup was being broadcast, and Thimphu had the only TV located at the swimming pool where I would practice my exercises. Late at night, we snuck out of the monastery and walked all the way to watch the TV broadcast along with fellow citizens in the surrounding area. Some town people would criticize us for being there involved in such a non-monk-like activity. We thoroughly enjoyed these escapades even though the game was aired at 1:00 AM, and afterward, we had the long trek back to the institute, often stopping along the way to take a reviving nap. We barely got back in time to attend morning prayer, followed by class. While attending class, we struggled to stay awake and giggled amongst ourselves behind the teacher's back, especially when one of us fell backward from sitting in the lotus position.

However, life took an unexpected turn when news reached me of my father's illness. Taking leave from school, I traveled to the village to bring my father to Thimphu for the necessary medical treatment. The diagnosis was devastating- throat cancer. For further assistance, my father was taken to Kolkata's renowned cancer hospital in India, accompanied by my brother-in-law. One month later, I traveled to join them by train, my first encounter with this mode of transport. With trepidation, I embarked on a day and night-long train journey filled with a mix of worry and pride. In Kolkata, the doctors provided a life expectancy estimate, and we returned to Bhutan. He was determined to make the most of our time together, pleading to return to his village, which we lovingly acquiesced for his comfort.

Upon my return to school from Kolkata, exams were pending, and my absence had put me at a disadvantage. Initially, my teachers advised me not to attempt them, suggesting instead to repeat the classes. However, remaining undeterred, I earnestly requested the chance to take the exams. The only subject I had missed was poetry, but I immersed myself in it and learned the rudiments. Poetry has always been one of my favorite subjects, and despite missing out on valuable classroom time, I took it upon myself to fully immerse myself in the subject. As soon as I returned to the room each day, I dedicated significant hours to studying, often pulling all-nighters and even sacrificing my own comfort by not even changing my clothes before bedtime. I wanted to ensure that I caught up on the missed lessons and thoroughly understood the topics at hand. Yet, during this intense period of study, I went through a traumatic experience when I discovered that I had contracted lice all over my body! It was a challenging time, both physically and mentally. However, I persevered, resolved the lice issue, and continued my efforts, undeterred by this setback.

While I was going through intense preparation for my upcoming exam, the saddest message was delivered to me that he had passed away. Amazingly, the day he died, I awoke in the middle of the night to the image of my father pulling on my bedclothes and pleading with me to awake. I stood up suddenly, causing my roommate to arouse from a deep slumber and ask me what happened. I told him right away that my father died, but he tried to reassure me that it was only a dream and could not be true. This proves the many inherent connections that a family has, which cannot be erased, and it also justifies the Buddhist belief in earthly and heavenly spirits. Being in a primitive environment, we had few technical luxuries, and the sole phone just recently installed on our campus was located in a teacher's house a short distance away. I stirred from my bed from a deep sleep and heard a student calling my name, Lopen Dodam (Bhutanese for captain), mentioning that there was a phone call for me. I responded, "I know, my father has died," and he said, perhaps out of respect, "I don't know what the phone call is about." Nevertheless, I went to the teacher's house, and as soon as I walked in, I told my teacher that I knew about my father passing away, as he came to me in the early morning. He was shocked and speechless temporarily, but he soon assured me with a heavy heart that it was true. Sadly, I was not able to return to my home village to attend the funeral, but I was able to offer butter lamps and gnomon (prayers) in various holy places. I believed that this would have satisfied my father's departed soul even better than attendance at the funeral. My aunt told me that my father's last wish on his dying bed was that I should continue with my education and not worry about him. He was selfless to the very end and manifested his deep love for me by wishing for me not to ignore my education and ultimate destiny.

I was pleased that my hard work had paid off in an unexpected manner, placing me at the top tier of my class, which I had maintained over the school years. Despite the difficulties and losses I faced, I managed to score exceptionally high in the poetry subject, thereby securing a place at the top of the class once again. This achievement assured me that my dedication and commitment to my studies had not been in vain. I genuinely believed that my performance in the poetry exam showcased my capability to excel in the subject despite the obstacles I encountered.

Chapter 3: Fond Memories

After completing my four-year course at Dodedrak Shedra, I felt privileged to have been selected for higher studies at Tango Buddhist College in 1998. Embarking on this new chapter in my educational journey filled me with both excitement and a competitive mindset. I remember with great admiration the renowned and departed scholar Lopen Kinley Gyeltsen, who served as our guiding light during our first year of the master's program. Enrolling at Tango was an enlightening experience, as our class consisted of nearly seventy students from diverse backgrounds, all coming together to aspire to academic achievement. The presence of several groups from different institutes made the learning environment vibrant and intellectually stimulating. Under the guidance of Lopen Kinley Gyeltsen and his team of sagacious teachers, we were constantly challenged to achieve our potential and excel in every discipline.

Lopen Kinley Gyeltsen's reputation for being strict and his exceptional teaching methods only added to the anticipation and nervousness among us new students. I vividly recall our very first day of class with him, followed by a unique ritual on the second day. Each morning before the class began, one student would be chosen to rehearse the lesson from the previous day, through a random draw. I can still feel the mixture of fear and excitement as we wait for our names to be pulled from the small container filled with the students' names. On that fateful day, it was my name, " Kuertoy Pema Thinley," that was called out. Initially, I felt reluctant, yet the thrill of the opportunity quickly overcame any doubts. I embraced the role of a teacher and approached the rehearsal with confidence, showcasing my academic prowess. To my delight, Lopen Kinley Gyeltsen applauded my efforts and jokingly remarked that I would one day be appointed as a Khenpo (instructor) in Sharchog (East), where I initially enrolled in the institution.

At Tango, I shifted my passion and interest from academic pursuits to focusing on writing songs for the movies and audio cassettes which began to grow in popularity during my third and fourth years. This newly found interest led me to interact with renowned entertainers within the Bhutanese music industry. I wrote over seventy songs, which were greatly appreciated by singers and movie producers. However, my dedication to this hobby led to a decline in my academic performance, particularly during exam time.

During this period, I had the pleasure of meeting an American doctor and his family from Alaska, and our friendship continued to blossom. It was during our conversations that my interest in learning English accelerated and I realized that being in an English-speaking environment would provide me with invaluable opportunities to improve my language skills and broaden my perspectives. Upon their return to America, I was elated to hear that they would be willing to invite me to their country to help me achieve my goals. Their generosity was truly amazing, and I couldn't express my gratitude enough for this remarkable opportunity.

I had dreams of exploring new horizons and seeking better opportunities, so I decided to embark on a journey to America. As I prepared to leave Bhutan, I jokingly told my sister, "Once I get there, you can ask me for money, and I'll ask how much fifty thousand ngultrum is worth." My sister laughed at my playful remark, thinking it was unimaginable for me to send such a substantial amount of money, especially in our humble circumstances where even five hundred ngultrums were considered a lot. (Ngultrum is the basic currency of Bhutan, 100 equaling one American dollar.)

The day finally arrived when I set on my route for America, filled with hope and determination. As I started adapting to my new life, I became aware of my family's struggles back home. My mother required care, and my brother-in-law, who had been supportive of me during my studies in Bhutan, was going through tough times. Remembering my promise to my brother-in-law, I began sending money to support my family. Despite having my own responsibilities in America, I couldn't bear to see my loved ones suffer. I knew that I had to help not only my immediate family but also my nieces and nephews, who needed assistance with education and basic needs.

Days turned into weeks, and weeks into months, and I dedicated myself to tirelessly supporting my family from afar. I studied and worked diligently to earn money and made use of every opportunity to uplift my loved ones. I prioritized their well-being, often neglecting my own needs and desires. However, with the growing number of nieces and nephews, it became overwhelming. The pressure of supporting the extended family started weighing heavily on me and sometimes I felt torn between my family responsibilities and the aspirations I had for myself. But despite the challenges, I understood the importance of family and worked tirelessly to ensure a good life for them, which resonated deeply with them.

Witnessing my unwavering support, my brother-in-law felt immense gratitude for my life-changing gesture.

My financial assistance helped him regain accountability, and our relationship grew stronger, based on mutual trust and support. As the years passed, I continued to work hard, always keeping family as my top priority. My continuous love and constant support made a tremendous difference in the lives of those I cared for, leaving an indelible mark on their hearts.

Through the ups and downs, I learned that supporting a large family can be challenging, but the fulfillment I felt by being there for my loved ones outweighed any burden. I understood that family was not just about blood relationships but caring for one another unconditionally. My journey from a small village in Bhutan to America was not just a tale of personal growth and ambition; it was a story of love, sacrifice, and a profound sense of duty toward family. My determination to provide for loved ones illustrated the power of selflessness and the impact that one person can have on the lives of many. And so, my story serves as a testament to the enduring strength of family bonds, reminding us that no matter where we are in the world, supporting and caring for our loved ones will always remain a fundamental part of our lives.

Chapter 4: Journey Awaits

As I prepared to embark on this life-changing journey, I gathered all the necessary documents; however, I needed an invitation letter from them, which was an essential requirement for my visa applications to the United States. They happily provided me with this crucial letter which enabled me to travel to important destinations. Upon receiving the invitation from them, I had an incredible experience that took place after I received their kind invitation. In anticipation of this life-changing adventure, my friend and I decided to partake in a traditional custom that is believed to welcome positive energy and good fortune on my journey. This custom involved a unique ritual performed in a sacred room called Goenkhang. I lit incense and prepared myself for what lay ahead, the usage of dice in a proscribed manner. To my absolute amazement and delight, the outcome of this custom surpassed all expectations. At the roll of the dice, it was as if fate smiled upon me. Three dice, perfectly aligned, formed a tower of good fortune – an auspicious sign. However, what truly left me awestruck was the fact that each of the three dice revealed a single dot, an occurrence that is typically seen only in the realm of royal personages. This preordained result filled me with a sense of karmic assurance as if it further foreshadowed the positive outcome awaiting me during this pivotal stage of my life. I might add that in a dream steps to achieve my new life were highlighted and thus relieved me of all doubt that this journey was preordained to occur. This sounds fantastic but nonetheless, I was determined to fulfill my destiny, as my dreams in the past almost always predicted favorable circumstances. And to this day, I ignore bad dreams for fear of their unfavorable outcomes.

I couldn't believe how fortunate and blessed I was to have experienced this profound chain of events. It was a powerful reminder of the extraordinary journey that lay ahead and the incredible opportunity that awaited me. I was filled with immense gratitude for this perfectly aligned start to my preparations, and I believed it augured well for the new chapter I would embark upon in my host's beautiful country.

A train ride was necessitated to the destination of New Delhi, India in order for me to obtain a tourist visa from the American Embassy. This legal obligation would propel me forward to a new realm of existence that I was eagerly awaiting. This process was arduous due to the fact that it was only several months after the tragic events of 9/11. Everybody applying was automatically rejected because of concern about terrorists reentering the United States. These circumstances did not deter me for a number of reasons. As depicted earlier in this story, I had a streak of good fortune which was delineated by the custom of tossing dice, and my episode of tossing was auspicious to a high degree. Before I left Thimphu my friends arranged for accommodations in New Delhi. The Bhutanese ambassador, Lonpo Dago Tshering, and his wife Aum Tshokey were gracious enough to invite me to stay at their home and provided transportation and driver to travel anywhere in New Delhi in grand comfort.

The next story involves a cast of characters that were highly beneficial to my acquiring the tourist visa from the American Embassy. While I was still residing with the Bhutanese ambassador I was preparing for an appointment at the American Embassy. To my utter amazement, my Dutch friend in Bhutan emailed me and advised me not to get an appointment yet as she would connect me to the ambassador's wife who was her friend. She said the wife of the ambassador was out of the country and I had to wait which amounted to an extra two months living in New Delhi. This was actually fortuitous as it allowed me to live with the Bhutanese ambassador and time spent studying and enjoying their company, as everybody at the embassy treated me so well.

Although the stay with my Bhutanese host was very pleasant I was losing confidence and became impatient to see results as there was no progress and I became despondent. I emailed an Australian friend in Sydney and asked her if she would sponsor me for a trip to her homeland. She readily agreed and sent me an invitation for immigration purposes. I applied and got an appointment at the Australian embassy which I received complete with an interpreter. So my request was approved and they retained my passport asking me to collect a visa five days later. But the very next day I was just roaming around in the Bhutanese embassy and people frantically looked for me to give me good news. Our ambassador had been contacted by the American ambassador to alert me to an appointment at

11:30 that same morning. My interpreter called the Australian embassy to cancel that visa and informed them that I would be visiting to collect my needed passport. It went smoothly and immediately I went to the American embassy to meet the ambassador's wife. It was a revelation to notice the extensive protection surrounding the American embassy, but my interpreter and I were able to enter without incident. We were greeted graciously by the ambassador's wife and offered coffee in the living room. She informed us that the embassy does not have the authority to issue the visa but she arranged for a meeting with the American consular at the Immigration Department within the same compound accompanied by their personal secretary. In my mind, I envisioned success in obtaining the visa so I was not disappointed as I interpreted this as a mere formality. I was greeted by the consular and offered tea. From this room, I could see a line of people who were rejected during the formal process – they were visibly shaken and crying pitifully. I felt blessed to have received such a warm welcome and be in the audience with these American officials. The consular interviewed me and asked me only one question - why I wanted to go to America, to which I responded I wanted to improve my English. He said there was a different process for that procedure so right away I changed the direction of the conversation and indicated I wanted to improve life skills. He took my passport and asked me to wait fifteen minutes after which he returned with my passport with a visa stamped.

Following is a new episode to share with you of the incredible journey to America filled with memorable encounters and heartwarming experiences that I will cherish forever. When I left New Delhi, the Bhutanese ambassador and his wife went above and beyond all expectations to ensure a smooth departure for me. They kindly arranged for their duty car, along with guards and a driver to drop me off at the airport. Their generosity truly touched my heart.

I boarded my flight and had a layover in London for about eight hours. It was during this time that a rather unique incident occurred. I was still dressed in my monk's robe and carrying my Drangen Bhutanese Guitar. As I sat in the airport's sitting area, people started approaching me and offering money. Although I couldn't understand much, I expressed my gratitude using the few words I knew. It was an interesting experience to have my limited vocabulary come in handy. However, there was one gentleman who seemed to be under the influence. Despite my attempts to refuse his money, he persistently came back until eventually disappearing to his designated gate for San Francisco. To my amazement, I counted the money gifts which amounted to $81. Thankfully, ten hours later, my flight departed, taking me closer to America.

During the flight, I found a seat next to a young Punjabi man who noticed that I struggled to communicate. Fortunately, he could speak Hindi, so he kindly guided me throughout our journey using the language. My broken Hindi, which I had picked up from a rickshaw driver in New Delhi, proved to be quite useful. This experience highlighted the value of knowing multiple languages, even if one is not proficient.

As we soared through the skies, crossing vast oceans, words cannot describe the overwhelming emotions I felt. I was filed with an indescribable mixture of happiness and excitement. When the majestic landscape of New York City came into view, it felt like stepping foot onto a different planet as the illuminated cityscape, with its towering buildings left me in awe.

Upon landing in NY, I went through the customs check and one particular officer showed great respect because of my monk's robe. She not only admired it but also took the time to write down her contact information and handed it to me, encouraging me to reach out to her in the future. Although I didn't have the opportunity to contact her, the gesture of warmth and acceptance made me feel incredibly welcome in America.

Finally, as I reached the airport's arrival area, I was warmly greeted by three individuals holding scarves in their hands. Among them were Aue Dotu and Aue Namgyel, and I must apologize for momentarily forgetting the name of the third person. They made sure my arrival was comfortable and graciously escorted me home. My host Aue Dotu had to leave early for work so I was eager to explore the neighborhood despite no knowledge of the surroundings in Queens. I was thrilled to come upon a soccer practice among professional athletes, and later found out they were the New York Red Bulls. After a little more exploration of my new found home city I returned back to my host's abode and gratefully prepared a typical Bhutanese dinner with ingredients brought from Bhutan. He was delighted to share the delicious meal and we enjoyed interesting conversations, including messages from his family which they entrusted me to deliver. His niece, Dechen Pem, a popular singer in Bhutan known as the "Queen of Pop" whom I wrote many songs for, extended hearty greetings to her beloved uncle, my gracious host.

A few days later I started my momentous journey to Alaska to visit and reside with my host family, which I had been joyously anticipating for many months. There was a transit stop in Seattle before my ultimate destination of Juneau, which caused some unforeseen complications. As I was going through the checkpoint, some officials searched me and questioned me about carrying any weapons or contraband. I misinterpreted their line of questioning and thought they asked if I had luggage, which I had. This was due to my lack of English language understanding. They were gesticulating towards my backpack but I kept on pointing to the luggage carousel saying "there there" the only phrase I could muster. They brought in an Asian employee and tried to have her interpret but to no effect. Finally, a police officer pantomimed the firing of a gun during my interrogation, and that's when I realized the line of questioning and I said "no, no" to much laughter on their part and great relief on mine. So they rushed me ahead to my flight as it was ready for departure and I was the only missing passenger. As soon as I boarded, the plane left and I was headed to my host family. It was amazing that the USA was so vast and I had no idea that there were so many miles of frontier within the nation.

We reached Juneau, Alaska, and at the airport, my host family awaited me with open arms and an offering of the traditional Bhutanese welcoming white scarf. I had reached my destination and was ready for new experiences which my family provided. They lived right next to the ocean and their house was adjacent to a living quarter for me. My space was a perfectly designed room that resembled a Buddhist temple with all the appropriate hangings. There were mounds of snow all around the area - obviously, Alaska was known for the cold winter weather and Juneau was no exception even though it was in the southern part of the state.

My first responsibility was enrolling in English classes and learning as fast as possible. The class consisted of only a few students but they were a diverse group of foreigners and the teachers were dedicated to our success. I befriended one teacher, Joanne Bloom, who provided me a house whenever I was in her area and was able to accelerate the learning process. My popularity grew and even the state senator, Kim Elton, invited me to provide the invocation at the Senate opening ceremony. I was their guest during the proceedings and was televised along with the others conducting business at this august arena of public affairs. Because of this publicity whenever I traversed the local streets people would stop their cars and welcome me to their homes. They never locked their doors and gave me permission to visit at any time whether they were home or not which gave me full confidence, realizing how safe this community was.

Chapter 5: Alaska

During my time in Alaska, I had some interesting and funny experiences and the opportunity arose to take an "English as a Second Language" course at the University of Alaska campus. With the help of my teachers, host, and newly minted friends, my English skills gradually improved, due to the fact there was a program specially tailored for my needs. I frequently visited Auke Bay Elementary School in order to gain confidence by teaching and interacting with the young students. They learned my national language Dzongkha (basically Bhutanese), and I taught them the Bhutanese national anthem and a little ditty "Kuzuzangpo Kuzuzangpo Zhugayla" which they were thrilled to learn.

One person who played a significant role in my progress was Dan Lesh, a fellow student at the University of Alaska. He became a close friend and provided me with a lot of support along the way. It's amazing how relationships can blossom in such a short period of time. One sport that was recommended to me by Dan was snow skiing which I actually had no practical experience with before. I had no idea how it was to be accomplished but I endeavored to do this on my own since I was introduced to this exotic sport. I thought there was a slope for beginners but before I had time to react I was jumping off the ski lift and barreled down the steep hill, not even able to see my friend or other skiers. Well, I thought it was up to me to succeed at this sport and I gained much confidence even after falling several times to the ground. When I rendezvoused with my friend Dan he could notice much improvement on my part and praised me profusely for my trying such an alien sport. When we left for home I met Dan at his car in the parking lot. I must confess at this point a humorous anecdote. Dan was an impoverished college student and his car was the source of much good ribbing between us for the fact that it hardly ran at all – he had to jumpstart it usually before it would even budge. We had many hearty laughs as a result and Dan was certainly an appreciative friend.

Juneau, the small and cozy town where I stayed was a delight. The sense of community and warmth was truly delightful. However, there were a few incidents that stood out, which I can't help but laugh about now. One evening, I was invited to have dinner at my teacher's daughter Lindsey Bloom's birthday celebration, along with Dan and some other friends. After the meal, they planned to head out to a bar and invited me along. Unfamiliar with the concept, I innocently asked them what a bar was, which apparently caught them by surprise. They all found my naïveté humorous! Many years later, probably twenty-two, I was corresponding with Lindsey and we reminisced about that evening. She chuckled about the fact that I didn't know what a bar is on Facebook and this brought back a flood of memories.

Around this time I was waxing romantic and looking for female companionship, and consequently, I met a beautiful American woman named Gloria who was working with AmeriCorps at the local library. She was thrilled to meet a Buddhist monk and eagerly helped me with my inquiries, stirring a conversation that developed into a close relationship. Years later, our closeness blossomed into something more intimate, and I will always be grateful for her help and empathy.

Another unforgettable moment occurred when Senator Kim Elton and his wife kindly invited me to their house for dinner. As soon as I entered, Kim took my jacket and hung it in the closet. They offered me a drink and proudly mentioned that it was home-brewed. To my dismay, the drink turned out to be wine. I had never tasted it before and didn't particularly enjoy it. In my attempt to express my preference, I inadvertently said, "It's not good." The couple politely laughed, understanding that my innocent comment was unintentional due to my language limitations.

Lastly, my host encouraged me to freely ride a bicycle during my stay, and I was ecstatic about that offer. Unfortunately, while I was going a bit too fast, I stumbled on some gravel and fell off the bike, leaving a noticeable scratch on my knee. Feeling embarrassed, I decided not to mention it to anyone.

My host family was very involved in updating and extending my tourist visa into a student visa and this required many steps which were not always pleasant to go through. My host mother Suzanne tried to change the visa to allow me to live in Oregon but this was not to transpire. We had to visit the local immigration office to be advised how to accomplish this feat. At first, the local official was uncooperative and surly, not wanting to help in any way. But then he discovered I was a monk and became more amenable to my needs by offering advice. Nothing could be done to ameliorate the situation but he did advise us to apply for an extension of six months so that I wouldn't end up in the undocumented category.

The time was rapidly approaching that I was to take leave to New York and it was a bittersweet moment in my life. My friends and host family secretly planned a farewell party for my impending departure and it seemed like all of Juneau attended the festivities. Many funny and endearing stories were recalled by the guests regarding my knowledge of modern American culture and the hilarity that ensued because of my lack of understanding of the quirks of society. It was also recalled the travel incident at the airport when I didn't comprehend the officials as they were grilling me for information concerning any weaponry on my person. Peals of laughter filled the room and the guests were very pleased to hear of my travel experiences. If you remember, I also had an interesting layover at Heathrow Airport in London, involving international passengers donating money just because of my monk robe; well the party guests were reminded of this incident and warmly embraced me for this retelling.These incidents may seem relatively minor, but they hold special memories for me. They remind me of the wonderful people I met and the unique experiences I had during my time in Alaska.

Chapter 6: New York

After a fond farewell with intentions of eventually returning, I was about to fly to New York the next day to seek a different life and explore all possibilities. A flight with only one layover in Chicago's O'Hare Airport took me to my final destination. I was prepared to work in the Big Apple and shed all vestiges of my previous Buddhist lifestyle. I was fortunate to be helped by the dearest Bhutanese man, Lopen Kinley known as Rueb Kinley, who met me at the airport and put me up in his house, for whom, I will forever be grateful. My brother-in-law's brother. Rinchen Norbu, was at that time living with him and I also owe him my sincere gratitude for his unwavering help.

The subway system can be quite intimidating, especially for the novice I was. I would like to relate to two stories that illustrate this point. The first one sounds pathetic from today's perspective but was nevertheless a source of frustration back when it occurred. I was returning home on the wrong train which took me on a confusing and roundabout trip. I didn't know which station to debark from and ended up in an endless loop all through the system, including the furthest stop in Long Island. Although some kind strangers showed me quickly in typical New York fashion how to navigate the system, I couldn't understand the mapping and the subway car became my home for the night. When I returned to my hosts' home early in the A.M., they were surprised to greet me and questioned with sympathy the reason for my tardiness. Out of embarrassment because of my prideful nature, I lied to them and concocted a story of me visiting a friend which they accepted.

The other story involves a bit of chicanery due to my subway card not being activated by the entry to the subway stop. Frustrated by the inconvenience, I jumped over the turnstile and hurried to the train. Lo and behold, I felt a pressure on my shoulder – the long arm of the law had placed his hand on me beckoning me to stop. Luckily he recognized my innocent nature as a newly minted resident and allowed me to proceed but nevertheless, I missed the train and waited patiently for the next train. Several months later I confided in a fellow Bhutanese this same story and he has never let me forget, reminding me jovially of that transformative experience.

I may be an accomplished chef now in 2023, but at this time in my New York time of life, I was quite naïve about American cuisine, especially a staple of this country's dietary intake – the hotdog. It was ubiquitous, especially in the middle of New York, where it originated, but I had an aversion to it for a particular reason. It had been in my presence many times and I suppose I should have participated in its unique delights, but I was under the mistaken impression that it was made from the meat of unfortunate dogs. It wasn't until much later that I finally partook in eating a hotdog, adding to my knowledge of worldly cuisine.

After investigating the lay of the land I immediately prepared for a new business. Aue Thinley Dorji, currently known as Tasha and is well known in social media to

Bhutanese people helped me to establish my roots for which I am still immensely grateful and remain on the friendliest of terms. He supplied me with a whole kiosk setup until I was able to procure my own supplies and products. This probably started me, although inadvertently on my trajectory toward my present-day business acumen. It soon became abundantly clear to me that I had to set up in Manhattan to start a livelihood of selling souvenirs/photographs on the busy streets, even though I was living in Brooklyn at the time. It was a hectic and cut-throat sort of business because every day, you had to wake up at 2:00 AM, gather all supplies, and compete for a spot on the street corner to function as a vendor. This was difficult, especially on the weekend. I developed quite a reputation as a feisty street competitor and confronted others wholeheartedly for a space to sell, thus earning a good amount of street smarts. Two competing vendors were not successful on their own and I took them under my wing so that they could have a modicum of income and self-respect, to which they were greatly appreciative.

I would like to share an interesting and unforgettable experience I had while working in a plastic utensil manufacturing warehouse in Delaware. As you know, after selling pictures in Times Square in New York, I was looking for a job change and found a job opportunity through a 3rd party agency. Upon accepting the position, I was delighted to learn not only were we provided a house to live in, but I also had the opportunity to lead a group of seven individuals. The agency offered me a slightly higher pay rate of $8 per hour compared to my friends, giving me my first taste of personnel management.

Working night shifts in the warehouse turned out to be quite challenging. We had to stand for eight hours, operating and keeping up with the machines while constantly moving our hands. After finishing our shift in the morning, we would rest during the day, cooking and having our meals together before retiring to bed, and preparing for our next work shift. While the job took its toll on my friends, leading some of them to feel worn out and complain, I found myself enjoying the work. My friends often mentioned that my cheerful demeanor and my willingness to sing and work happily motivated them not to give up. It was heartening to know that my positive attitude made a difference in their experience.

However, during our time at the warehouse, we encountered an unexpected incident. Another group, also consisting of Tibetans like us, worked alongside us and shared the same house. One day, one of them encountered a payment issue with the agency and decided to involve the police. They informed us that the police had been called and advised us to hide, as we were undocumented immigrants who had overstayed our visas from Bhutan. Our fear of being detained and sent back to Bhutan led us to view the police as immigration personnel. As a result, we panicked and hid ourselves in the middle of a cornfield near our house, striving to keep our distance from the authorities. We walked cautiously through the cornfield, fearful of being noticed by the police. To our surprise, accidentally we ended up walking in front of the police but we were surprised they were not interested in our predicament, allowing us to breathe a sigh of relief and laugh at our own innocence in the whole situation. This incident remains etched in my memory, serving as a constant reminder of how innocent and vulnerable we were at the time. Even now, wherever I notice similar emotions in some of my foreign employees, I am reminded of that day and strive to provide support and guidance to help them through their own challenges. Despite the unique experience at the warehouse, we were only able to endure two months of demanding work before returning to New York. Although short-lived, it was a period of growth and unforgettable moments that I carry with me to this day. This is one of the unforgettable chapters of my journey.

To my detriment, at this time in my life, I became fascinated by the challenge and glitzy atmosphere of gambling in the casinos of Atlantic City, New Jersey. Coordinated with my Bhutanese friends, we boarded a bus and were excited to head to the casinos, with hard-earned money in our pockets and hope in our minds. We arrived and excitedly went to our rooms, ready to explore the den of iniquity. The atmosphere was intoxicating for most of us but there were a few experienced ones who looked after us and recommended what to do. I only knew how to play poker so I made a beeline to the poker tables and commenced the betting. The first couple of hours I was ahead and made approximately $9K, but this did not satisfy my desire, and continued on hoping to accumulate a fortune.

Unfortunately, this was not to materialize and I ended up losing $4200 and not a cent to spare. I went back to my room and enjoyed a romantic evening with a female friend. Experience gained and a lesson learned. This sated my curiosity about the high roller crowd, and I didn't relive this lifestyle until many years later in Las Vegas, which I will delve into in a later paragraph. Luckily I still had a return bus ticket to New York, went back Friday night directly to the street kiosk on my secured spot, napped a few hours on a chair, ready to sell more souvenirs as the sun rose above Times Square – this indeed is the life of an industrious immigrant enjoying the ups and downs of life in the US. All day and all night Saturday, this procedure was repeated until a gang fight started and disturbed my nap, forcing me to run for safety but keeping a close eye on the kiosk, anxious that it would be stolen. After an hour, relative peace returned in the "city that never sleeps", allowing my business to continue. Surprisingly, even in the dark early hours of the morning, people were wandering by and purchasing my merchandise. Usually, at this point, my secret paramour would visit with lunch and pleasant conversation and we enjoyed a few moments together. Because of this intense nonstop schedule I was able to recoup my losses incurred at Atlantic City and returned home after two days and nights, none the worse for wear.

I was continually contacting the employment agency in Chinatown, unsatisfied with the souvenir sales job and searching for better opportunities. While at the agency, I joked with them about finding a "mommy-sitting" job which amused them very much. I befriended a Chinese lady and we developed a warm relationship. She recommended a position in an Asian fast-food restaurant at the West Nyack Palisades Mall, a live-in job that provided me with housing and transportation back and forth to work. On my day off, I would explore the community. I came across an announcement for an English as a Secondary Language course offered at Rockland County High School. I was thrilled for this opportunity to further my chances for success. Early in the morning, I took the bus to the course before work started at 10:00, which suited my situation perfectly. Since my English skills were very limited, I was placed in the lowest level, but quickly improved to the point of understanding much better. Because of my propensity to help others, I called friends and notified them of this opportunity to work at the mall. My work experience was rated exemplary by my boss and this led to my leading the whole team which resulted in my boss happily accepting my friends and thus improving the profitability of the family business. Two of my friends arrived and we lived happily together in the apartment sharing a common bond of hard work and new horizons. I was able to transcend my own quotidian struggles and offer a bit of solace to other Bhutanese. There were some minor disagreements concerning pay with the owners which led to us quitting and accepting more lucrative positions next door with an Indian gentleman. It was awkward but necessary for all of our advancement. He appointed me the manager of his Philly Cheesesteak carryout establishment, which only lasted several months due to the fact that he was a gambler and lost all of his investments because of that pernicious habit. I should have warned him!

Okay, back to the streets again of Times Square and competing for valuable spaces to sell. This continued for a couple of months until I received an offer to come down to Baltimore, a city I was not familiar with – details below. Delightfully my English teacher from Alaska, Joanne

Bloom, contacted me about visiting New York on a business trip. She arrived the next week and we met with me acting as the tour guide and she completely enjoyed the sights. She was so proud of my improved English and the fact that I showed her around the city, which completely enchanted her.

One incident that highlights the many twists and turns in my complicated life involves a trip to Vermont via Albany with the Darla family, whom I befriended in Alaska. They invited and chaperoned on a trip to the upstate picturesque town of Newport, New York. From there we journeyed to Vermont on a ferry that carried people and cars, enjoying the scenery and fresh air along the way. This episode surprised and delighted me very much because I had never ridden a ferry before in my life, only heard about them in Alaska. I remained in Vermont for two weeks and met a woman who became infatuated with me, but unfortunately, I couldn't reciprocate the feelings and felt bad for her but she understood and we remained friends. To this day she still writes and communicates with me about the fun times we had during a formative time of my life. We attended services at a quaint little church and I was subsequently asked to officiate along with the local pastor in an invocation. On a side note, the Darlas were aware of a problem I was experiencing at the time with the expiration of my tourist visa and endeavored to solve the problem by collaborating with the church's immigrant services office, but there was no success.

Nevertheless, we were able to enjoy ourselves and forget the minor visa setback by participating in wondrous winter activities including ice skating and a very momentous bonfire. At this point, we were invited to a farmer's estate for dinner and a pleasant rest. When I entered the barn and reveled in the rural smells of manure and hay I was totally transported back to my childhood in Bhutan, reminiscent of early days of cow herding with my parents. That evening we had an authentic farmer's dinner of fresh ingredients out of the garden, including cheese and chicken.

On the return trip, I was sent with two young men who were friends of the Darlas and traveling back to the Big Apple. At first, we had an uneventful time for the first half of the journey, but then we came upon an internal Albany checkpoint that suddenly proclaimed itself in striking letters. All vehicles were stopped and checked by immigration authorities, and finally, we were next in line and ready to be scrutinized, with all our documents at the ready. As you'll remember my visa was in the process of being extended for an additional six months, but I had on me only the expired one attached to my passport. They invited me into the office for further investigation and as soon as I walked in, I witnessed many foreign detainees pleading and crying related to various documentation discrepancies. At first, I was a little nervous but silently prayed to the Buddhist yogi, my lineage's revered figure, Zhabdrung Rinpoche, which filled me with much solace as it erased all foreboding feelings. Even though an official, one of the young macho officers tried to scare me by saying "You know what's going to happen if you don't have proper documentation" and other menacing quips, I was not easily intimidated and responded "No problem, I have a beautiful country to return to" and remained stalwart. Many ideas were churning in my mind about possibly being deported, but only in terms of planning not desperation, as a blanket of peace descended upon me. This conversation interested an older, wiser officer who joined us and inquired about my monk existence, captivated by the robe I was wearing and was sincerely interested in my predicament. I am not sure but because of his calm demeanor and genuine empathy, he may have been the reason for the final resolution of this minor blip in my journey. My newly minted friends came to my rescue and peppered the officials with questions related to my detention. Using outdated fax machines the process for submitting my visa of course was delayed and left me with the old visa, causing a waiting period at this local office. After receiving confirmation from central headquarters, they handed the documents back to me and wished me luck.

An acquaintance of one of my Alaskan friends, Monica Ravin, was truly a godsend, as she introduced me to many aspects of city life, from restaurants to even cinemas and other cultural amenities. Eventually, she invited me to live in her apartment and there I remained helping her with everyday activities up until the moment I moved to Baltimore. At her apartment, she threw a Thanksgiving gathering for all of my Bhutanese friends and we thoroughly enjoyed ourselves. She will always be remembered as a gracious person to whom I am deeply indebted. After moving to Baltimore I traveled back to New York when she was in the hospital giving birth to beautiful twins, a boy and a girl who are currently in college. We remain dear friends and whenever we talk she is so proud of my achievements knowing of the arc of my peripatetic existence.

Chapter 7: Further Adventures

As has been mentioned earlier, I spent the summer selling pictures on the streets of New York City. However, with the freezing winter approaching, I knew it was time for a change and that's when I came across an interesting opportunity at a job agency in Chinatown. It was a waiter training job at a Japanese restaurant in Baltimore, so, intrigued by the idea of gaining experiences I decided to give it a try and traveled to Maryland's largest city.

To my surprise, when I arrived at the restaurant and introduced myself, I discovered that my cousin was already working there as a waiter – what a small world! It was a heartwarming moment to see a familiar face in a new environment. The owner of the restaurant kindly provided me with accommodation upstairs, making my transition to Baltimore much smoother.

I started my job training the next day and things were going well, and while serving customers, I overheard some people talking about a popular and sophisticated nightclub nearby. Captivated by the idea and eager to meet new people, I shared my excitement with my cousin and decided to visit the club after work. There was a feeling of manifest destiny on my own personal level to fulfill a so-called "appointment" regarding that evening. What would ensue I had no idea, but something was pushing me forward.

On my third day, after the shift, I headed towards the club while my cousin was taking some time to take a shower and get changed. However, I found it challenging to navigate to the destination and ended up standing in the same spot for a while, feeling a bit lost and blind toward the outside world. It was at this moment that a kind gentleman, who is now like a father to me, approached me. I asked him for directions to the famous Red Maple Club, not realizing that I was standing right in front of it. He laughed at my obliviousness but struck up a conversation with me. Discovering that I was from Bhutan, a Buddhist country, he was thrilled as he himself had practiced meditation for many years. I was pleasantly surprised by his knowledge of Bhutan and his awareness of worldly and spiritual concepts. Most people I encountered at that time in my life had no clear or even meager understanding of Bhutan and Buddhism in general, so I was enchanted by his scope of understanding. We had a wonderful chat with me employing my broken English to engage further, and he cooperated to the best of his ability to keep up the lively conversation. He mentioned introducing me to his partner, who is now a grandfather figure to me.

We exchanged contact information, and true to his word, the next day they both visited the restaurant where I worked. They invited me to their country home for dinner, and I gladly accepted. The evening was filled with delightful conversation, laughter, and warmth, with a cozy fireplace adding to the ambiance. As we chatted, they showed a genuine interest in my life, asking about my hobbies and plans. It was during this conversation that I shared my desire to study and earn a degree. This revelation seemed to inspire them, and without hesitation, they offered to sponsor my education.

The following day, my new father figure accompanied me to register for English as a Second Language (ESL) classes at the Baltimore City Community College (BCCC), initially at the English Language Learner (ELL) and culminating in the more advanced English as an Additional Language (EAL) category. I was outperforming even the native-speaking students who were completing their GED studies. My parents were impressed on a daily basis with my achievements in my studies, and my increasing command of the language was noticeable while propelling me forward to a more advanced curriculum. I completed all beginning courses inherent to GED completion, so the next level was attending the two-year college level at BCCC for my Associate Degree in General Studies, from which I eventually graduated with the highest honors. During this time I became interested in the sciences and focused diligently on the healthcare field taking chemistry, biology, anatomy and physiology, microbiology, and sociology. These courses were extremely challenging since they encompassed a combined lecture and lab format. Since my memorization skills were acute I had no trouble in the lab part, but the lecture was almost alien because of the unique nature of these courses. Undaunted because of my hunger for knowledge I rose to the level of top student, which led to an incident totally unworthy of professor behavior. After two tests with 100% performance, my

Biology teacher took me aside and accused me of cheating, so he separated me from the other top students in order to satisfy his misguided curiosity. This did not discourage me the least, instead, I was getting excited to prove to him my competence in the subject. The next four tests were administered with me in my new seating arrangement, and true to form I excelled in all tests, performing 100%. At first, he did not comment, but after the third test, he approached me and apologized profusely. I said that there was no need for an apology since I appreciated his instruction and enjoyed his class and having him as a professor. This affected him so profoundly that he even teared up noticeably. Following the final exam and receiving an A+, he emailed me an official apology which delighted me completely. It expressed, "Dear Pema – I am glad you enjoyed having me as an instructor, and I enjoyed having you as a student as well. Again, I want to apologize for in any way accusing you of "cheating" off of the other student. For what I came to realize as the semester progressed was how truly intelligent you, yourself are". As a person raised and educated in Buddhist philosophy, I valued and respected the teacher-student dynamic, and appreciated his dedication in educating his students.

With the built-in tutors at home, it was inevitable that I would accomplish my goals. Daddy would help me with English and History, while Grandpa would instruct me in Mathematics. They would both grill me in Biology and related courses It was a dream come true for me. I attended my classes with enthusiasm, and my parents, who had purchased a condo in a prestigious high-rise building, encouraged me to stay there. While they resided in the country home, I moved into the luxurious condo and continued my studies and work routine.

They even surprised me with a bicycle to commute to school and work. They would visit me on weekends, taking me out for meals and showing me the joys of the city. I am extremely grateful for all the opportunities they have provided me, and rather than becoming spoiled, I viewed it as a chance to make the most out of my life by continuing to work hard and appreciating every experience that came my way.

As an expression of love and appreciation I have written a poem dedicated to my parents celebrating our lives together:

ༀ། །ལས་དང་སྨོན་ལམ་བཟང་པོས་ཕྱུན་ཚིག་ཏུ་འདུས་པའི།།

ལྷག་བསམ་རྣམ་པར་དཀར་བའི་ཕྱུང་སེམས་ཀྱི་ཕ་མ།།

བྱམས་བརྩེ་སྐྱོ་བ་བཪ་རྟེན་ཅན་ཕ་མ་ལས་ལྷག་ཚུལ།།

ལན་རེ་དྲན་ཚེ་མིག་ནས་མཆི་མ་རེ་འཐྱུང་ངོ།།

Brought together by good prayers and aspirations - the parents (guardians) who are of exceptionally pure affection and kindness, tear drops roll down from my eyes when I think of the love and the care you showered upon me, more than my own parents,

སྟོབས་འབྱོར་ལྷ་དང་མཉམ་པའི་ཨ་རི་ཡེ་ཕྱོགས་ལ།།

རང་རེའི་མི་ཚེ་སྐྱོང་བའི་དང་ཚུལ་ལ་བསམ་ཚེ།།

ཚོས་བཟང་ལྷ་ཡི་མདུན་སར་སྐྱེབས་པ་དང་འདྲ་བའི།།

བསམ་བརྗོད་བྲལ་བའི་དགའ་སྐྱིད་ཚད་མེད་ཅིག་ཕར་བྱུང་།།

When I reflect upon the days I spent in America - the nation at par with the gods in terms of power and abundance, a boundless sense of joy, beyond words and thoughts, develops within my mind, as if I reached the celestial realm where Lord Indra teaches the Dharma.

ཁར་རྗེ་དབང་ཐང་བསོད་ནམས་ཀུང་འཛོམས་པའི་མཐུ་ལས།།

ཕ་མ་དངོས་ལས་ལྷག་པའི་དྲིན་ཆེན་གྱི་འོག་ཏུ།།

ལོ་ངོ་བཅུ་བཀྱད་རིང་དུ་དགའ་སྐྱིད་ལ་རོལ་བའི།།

བགའ་རྟེན་རྟེས་དྲན་དུས་སྟོན་བརྩི་བ་ནི་དགའ་ཞུང་།།

Through the power of convergence of luck, fortune, and merit, I have spent eighteen years of my life in great comfort and happiness,

Under the care of benevolent guardians who are of greater kindness than my parents, and as I celebrate the moment of remembering their gratitude, it gives me a great sense of joy.

དྲིན་ཅན་ཁྱེད་ཀྱི་རྣམ་དཀར་བགའ་དྲིན་གྱི་ཕྱུང་པོ།།

མི་ཚེ་ཉིས་འཕྱུད་རྒྱབ་རྲང་གནཞལ་བ་ནི་མི་ཕོད།།

ཡིན་ནའང་རྩ་དང་བླ་མར་གསོལ་བ་ཞིག་བཏབ་པས།།

དྲིན་ཅན་སྐུ་ཚེ་བརྟན་པའི་སྨོན་ལམ་ཞིག་ཞུའོ།།

If I were to measure the amount of wholesome gratitude I owe you, my benevolent guardians for life after life, it can't still be measured,

But, by supplicating to the enlightened masters and deities, I pray that you have a long life, my dear guardian of immense gratitude.

སྐྱེ་བ་འདི་ནས་བཟུང་སྟེ་ཚེ་རབས་ཀྱི་བར་དུ།།

རང་ཅག་པ་བུའི་འབྲེལ་བ་ཡུན་རིང་དུ་བསྐྱངས་ནས།།

མཐར་ཐུག་བྱང་ཆུབ་དས་པར་མཉམ་ཅིག་ཏུ་བསྒྲོད་པའི།།

སྨོན་ལམ་འདེབས་ལ་སྐུ་དང་བླ་མ་ཡིས་དགོངས་ཞིག།

From this life, in all our lifetimes, may we be born as a family for a long time.

And ultimately attain enlightenment together. May this prayer of mine be considered by enlightened deities and masters.

Chapter 8: Mistaken Identity

Once upon a downtown Baltimore time, on a Friday evening in September 2009, I found myself in the midst of a thrilling adventure with my friends. It was my prime time to hang out and we decided to visit the notoriously energetic nightclub called Power Plant. Little could I have realized that this night would take an unexpected twist.

As we made our way through the crowded club, something peculiar caught my attention. Perhaps it was my physique, which happened to be in great shape at the time, or maybe it was the mustache that adorned my upper lip. Whatever the reason, people began to mistake me for a popular Filipino boxer named Pacquiao. At first, I tried to correct their misunderstanding, explaining that I was not Pacquiao. However, my words fell on deaf ears as the enthusiastic crowd grew larger, surrounding me and eagerly posing for pictures. It seemed that no matter what I said, they were convinced that I was their beloved boxer. Amused by the situation, my mischievous friend Bart jokingly exclaimed, "Yay, Paquioa!" To my surprise, this only served to reinforce their belief that I was the famous boxer. People lined up to take pictures with me, even following me into the restroom for snapshots. As the night wore on and our spirits soared, we decided to continue the charade. Bart's playful comment had unintentionally solidified their conviction, and we couldn't help but have some fun with it. However, in the midst of our revelry, an unexpected performer took the stage, stealing the spotlight - Vanilla Ice.

In the blink of an eye, I found myself on stage alongside Vanilla Ice, who announced me to the crowd as "Pacquiao," perpetuating the misconstrued identity and sealing my fate. The audience erupted with excitement, and their cheers fueled my enthusiasm. As Vanilla Ice and I posed for pictures and I pretended to throw punches at the famous singer the crowd shouted encouragements. The night was filled with laughter and jubilation, and though no smartphones or social media existed at the time, people had brought their traditional cameras along. Unfortunately, I hadn't thought to bring one myself. I only managed to get one blurry picture on my flip phone which I carry on me to this day to show other people. As pictures were taken, some kind strangers showed me the photographs they had captured on film, giving me the chance to relive those surreal moments.

Despite the potential for broadcast on the news, I felt a sense of relief as the night drew to a close. The club adventure, fueled by mistaken identity and mixed-up names, became a memorable tale that my friends and I would share for years to come. The world may never know the true identity of that Pacquiao doppelganger, but it doesn't matter, because the amazement and merriment we experienced would forever be etched in our hearts.

One memory that reverberates is a beautiful evening at Tabrizi's restaurant where I found myself alone and enjoying the delightful atmosphere next to the Baltimore harbor. Little did I suspect the evening was going to take an unexpected turn. As fate would have it I crossed paths with a friendly, big, and strong young man who turned out to be a professional football player from Ohio. He was visiting his parents in the building where I lived and he approached me with a warm smile and offered me a drink. We engaged in conversation and soon enough, another acquaintance from the building joined us. The three of us formed an instant connection and decided to spend the rest of the evening together. They introduced me to a popular mixed drink called the 150 shot which I had never tried before. Feeling adventurous, I agreed to give it a try.

As soon as I downed the shot a wave of intoxication overwhelmed me. The whole floor seemed to shift as though I was experiencing a whirlwind. Undeterred, my new friends suggested we continue the night at Iguana Cantina, a lively bar club. I agreed and off we went. At the club, our football player friend's charm drew the attention of every woman in the establishment and I couldn't help but let slip his true identity, revealing his secret to a few intrigued individuals. Despite his wish to maintain anonymity, the cat was out of the bag. As the night progressed, the effects of the alcohol intensified, and I found myself completely inebriated. Fortunately, my friends ensured my safety and brought me back home. When I eventually woke up in my bed, I was surprised to see my grandpa sitting beside me. My parents usually stayed in our country home and were not around the condo often, but my grandpa had come in the middle of the night, worried about my well-being. His concern and presence reminded me of just how much my family cared for me. The bond between us has never faded and we continuously enjoy each other's company. The memories of their love and care remain affectionately in my heart to this day and tears well up in my eyes as I recall those precious moments of genuine concern for one another.

My first full-time professional local government job was as a park ranger for the Baltimore City government. I obtained this position because one of my customers at the restaurant where I was working was a highly positioned administrator for the Baltimore City government. She encouraged me to apply for an opening position in the local Park Service Department, which had just been newly created and there were vacancies for thirteen people, but seventy applicants showed up for the positions. Naturally, I was eager to apply and ready for a new adventure in a different field of endeavor. I was selected for an interview but before I went I contacted my friends at Tango, a place I continue to hold dearly, for some long-distance support in the form of a ritualistic Buddhist ceremony. I was confident in pursuing this city government position but in turmoil knowing there would be tough competition. When I arrived for the interview, many applicants were already there so I quietly took a seat. To my surprise, I was the first one called into the office where three employees were sitting waiting to ask questions. I had no fear or hesitation and related to them in a confident manner. This impressed them and I was hired on the spot, unlike all the other applicants. Although my language skills were still developing, the managers who conducted the interview were impressed with my mental abilities and my physical fitness for the job. I left the office with full gratitude to my beloved Tango friends for offering prayers and encouragement.

It became apparent that I would need a mode of transportation for the park ranger job since I would be stationed throughout the city and everybody was heavily dependent on cars. I went to a car lot with my dad and grandpa and we perused the vehicles on the lot. Lo and behold, a Buick La Crosse was waiting for us on the lot almost pleading with us to choose it, not surprisingly because this was my dad's favorite brand of car. It was silver with a burgundy interior, and to me, it symbolized the great American dream, since Buick is one of the oldest companies, and incidentally started by an immigrant. It was love at first sight with this behemoth of a car and I was ready to roll even though I only possessed a learner's permit with little driving experience under my belt. We traveled back home as a convoy and ceremoniously parked my new possessions carefully in the underground parking lot of our building. That night we celebrated by going to a gourmet restaurant resplendent in the new Buick as if a chariot delivering me to new heights of luxury and privilege. Of course, I needed more practice at maneuvering such a valuable asset, so Grandpa continued to instruct me on driving, and actually took me to a vast parking lot of a Walmart next to the water at Port Covington and set up driving cones to simulate a training course. One day out of excitement to drive, but not a very logical step, I absconded with the Buick and visited my dearly departed friend, Pemba Sherpa, appropriately nicknamed "Happy" among all friends. I drove over the busy city roads trying unsuccessfully to connect with the proper route and ended up, just like a scene from a comical movie, on an unfamiliar highway, US 95. Not knowing what to do I persevered along the way and luckily ended up at a gas station near our country home in the suburbs. I called my dad who was at work, and he instructed me to remain there since it was just minutes from our second home. He arrived and I followed him home we left the car with Grandpa driving me back to the city home and ultimately to ESL class. I was almost late for the important instruction.

My duties and responsibilities as a park ranger were multifaceted and took me to all parts of Baltimore. I was privileged to work with such highly educated individuals who answered many of my questions as we rode our bicycles on trails through all of the parks we were assigned to. There was a sad development at this time in my life. In my fourth year (a total of seven years with city government) there was a downturn in the city budget which necessitated laying off a majority of the park rangers. I was not included in this decision but was saddened by the departure of many of my fellow workers. In my fifth year, I was assigned to my most consequential position at the Washington Monument, not to be confused with the more recent construction in Washington D.C. This is where I learned that Baltimore's monument is actually the first one erected to commemorate our founding father. As I mentioned earlier, this job was consequential because I was able to study an array of subjects and also exercise by running up and down the approximately 228 steps during my frequent breaks to increase my stamina and overall health. Most visitors to the monument were completely worn out after completing one episode of climbing. Many of my Bhutanese friends who were medical doctors and studying for a Master's in Public Health at Johns Hopkins University would jokingly refer to the monument as "Pema's temple".

Among all the parks we patrolled, Carroll Park had a notorious reputation, and yet my partner and I were required to ride through trail patrol on bicycles provided by our organization. We had exerted ourselves on our rounds and decided to rest for a moment with my partner further away. I got in my personal car and rested with the bike next to it, closing my eyes for some needed refreshment. I was sitting there and suddenly I awakened to a surprise. My bike was missing and I noticed that someone was riding it into the distance on the road. I started my car and pursued the thief, with my coworker close behind. My anger was aroused and I almost ran the man over but instead controlled the situation by blocking him off. He was making excuses for his poor behavior, by stating that the bike was just abandoned, a poor excuse for an obviously criminal act. I lectured him on exhibiting such behavior with the caveat that it could have been much worse. He departed and I was left with the responsibility of filling out an incident report at park headquarters.

A jarring incident that occurred a few weeks later involved me driving my beloved Buick, carrying two coworkers, Elizabeth and Carlos on the way to lunch on Coldspring Lane. I was motoring along and came to an intersection with a green light, when suddenly an irresponsible SUV driver came barreling through the opposing side street, going through the red light and clipping us on the side. Luckily there were only minor injuries, but her car pushed us 100 yards and completely totaled my car. The devastation was such that I had to crawl out of the far passenger window with no other alternative for egress. The police were notified and arrived in due time for a traffic incident report. The lady who caused the accident was belligerent and tried to blame me for the turmoil, but her subterfuge did not fool the attending officer and she was swiftly detained. An ambulance came and took the three of us to the emergency room at Mercy Medical Center, where we were observed for a couple of hours, no outward or internal injuries were detected, and released. A police report was issued and I contacted a lawyer friend who was able to transact a nominal recovery for the accident.

At this time, I had been married to a friend I met in Alaska who was very instrumental in my adapting to the country. She corresponded with me, expressing a romantic interest, and eventually came to Baltimore where we conducted our nuptials. However it was not meant to be, and after four years we agreed to an amicable divorce, going our separate ways, but remaining friends. She still has a place in my heart, as she was instrumental in acclimating me to a new environment.

Being an all-American at this point, I was itching for a new mode of transport and went with a fellow park ranger/friend Carlos to the local Chevrolet dealer, due to the fact that he was very knowledgeable about cars. My future car was to be the complete opposite of the Buick, in the form of the classic sports car Camaro. It was sitting sparkling in the showroom lights, with the windows rolled down, beckoning me to take it home. Carlos was joking with me that this transaction would never materialize, as this was almost too good to be true. I said, almost in an innocent manner, "I want that car" but he said, "That car is too expensive". I said, "Let me call my Dad, what is the car called." Carlos told me the name of the car, but when I called my dad I mispronounced it and said Camaro with an emphasis on the middle syllable, to which he laughed and said OK. My dad arrived, eager to witness the sports car which he had always admired throughout his life. He had owned a Corvette in the past and was well aware of the fun I would be experiencing, driving this all-American icon. We completed all the paperwork while I remained in a haze of wonderment and then proceeded to drive home. You can imagine how careful I was driving the Camaro home after all the circumstances of the past several weeks.

Because of this muscle car paired with the new body of muscles I developed, many girls were instantly attracted to me especially seeing the upscale condo I resided in overlooking the downtown skyline of Baltimore. They were entranced with all the physical and automotive musculature, and didn't even mind my pitiful ugly face! Many girls went through my condo as if it was Grand Central Station, but few remained and I was still single for some time.

I would like to shed some light on the early development of my business acumen. While working for Baltimore City Parks, an idea germinated in my mind propelling me to start a business, with generous input from my cousin Sonam Dorji, who currently lives in Queens, New York. We opened a kiosk business in the Baltimore Inner Harbor promenade specializing in knock-off handbags and wallets and a second location in the building showcasing a variety of perfumes. One other store was at the Harford Mall, tended to by an employee. These products were quite popular at that time and we successfully exploited the opportunity to our advantage. Our merchandise originated from New York and on several occasions, we had to drive there for replenishment while Sonam managed the three stores. Due to youthful exuberance, whenever I was stationed there on the weekends and days off from my main job, a party would develop and we ended up escorting young ladies who were also admirers of our product home to a bacchanalian episode. This sequence of events became quite an ongoing theme since we mixed business with pleasure at any possible moment.

Another major part of my life involved the meeting and eventual marriage to a Bhutanese visitor who landed at Dulles Airport intending to study at the University of Maryland's main campus, College Park. I was acquainted with her cousin who lived in New York, who picked her up at Dulles and delivered her to my place at Harborview condo. I took it upon myself to assist her by treating her and her cousin to dinner, and later driving her to College Park. My then-girlfriend, a Vietnamese college mate of mine, then drove all of us to her host family in College Park, said our goodbyes, and returned to Baltimore, but not before exchanging contact information to maintain a friendship. Over time, our bond strengthened and we continued a long-distance relationship as friends over the phone. She decided to drop her master's program classes and went to live in New York to work. She confided in me about the difficult circumstances of leaving two young children in Bhutan with their father. I was sympathetic to her plight and became more attached to her through the comforting process. After a week she called me and requested a favor – to retrieve her possessions and store them at my condo, which I gladly did. The ensuing weeks precipitated romantic feelings and I broke up with my girlfriend but no hard feelings happened. Through an odd twist of events, she notified me of her Bhutanese friend who was visiting Washington, D.C., and asked me if her friend could visit me. I acquiesced and met her friend over the phone, arranging her arrival. Spectacularly, Dorji (my future wife) decided to arrive a day earlier than her friend, and we pursued a romantic tryst. This was to become the beginning of my second marriage, which yielded a beautiful child, Zoya Zumsel, who to the present day remains the apple of my, Daddy's, and Grandpa's eye. I owe a great deal of gratitude to my parents, Grandpa and Daddy, who faultlessly provided for me and my extended family. Because of the help received by my parents, we never had to worry about money matters or a place to call home. They lovingly babysat Zoya and tended to her at any time necessary, partially due to the fact that at this point we lived in two condos just one floor separating our happy abodes. I was heavily engaged in my college studies and full-time work, and our living arrangement was ideal for all members of the family. This comfortable living arrangement occurred seamlessly while Dorji and I resided at Harborview, without any bills to worry about, even minor bills such as phone usage.

A few years ago, I finally reached a significant milestone in my life. After years of hard work and dedication, I successfully completed my education and accomplishments, and with it came the decision to buy a house of my own, an abode in which my family and I could create lasting memories. After careful consideration, I set my sights on a charming three-story townhome just up the street from my parents' condo. The location was perfect, allowing us to stay close to our loved ones while still enjoying privacy and independence. The process of turning the house into a home didn't take long to turn our new townhome into the epicenter of joy and laughter. With each passing day, we created cherished moments and built a strong foundation for my family. As time went by, opportunities seemed to knock on the door once again. One day, a four-story townhome adjacent to my parents' house was put up for sale. Its most enticing feature was its breathtaking view of the water. Spellbound by the possibilities, I decided to seize the chance to provide an even better living environment for my family. The thought of living next door to my parents, with the tranquil waves lapping against the shore just steps away, instantly filled me with excitement. It didn't take long for me to make up my mind that I was going to make this new house our home.

The process of purchasing and moving into the four-story townhome was a whirlwind of activity. We bade farewell to our old home, turning it into rental income, as it was filled with fond memories we still embraced the new chapter of our lives. The waterfront property offered a serene and picturesque backdrop that captured our hearts.

With each floor offering its unique charm and mesmerizing views, our new home quickly became a sanctuary, a place where we could relax, unwind, and appreciate the beauty of the neighborhood of Island Walk. Living so close to my parents proved to be a blessing as well. Family dinners and gatherings became regular occurrences, and our bond strengthened with each passing day. My daughter and stepson, later joined by my stepdaughter, grew up surrounded by love, and a close-knit family embraced as one of their own.

However, Dorji and my differences became apparent after some years of marriage, but we both persevered for the sake of our daughter Zoya and continued living together until the relationship became irreconcilable. This dissolution was prompted by my decision to separate, with us both agreeing to the separation and terms of the co-parenting agreement. With uttermost care, we did not let our child be hurt, and I even provided funds for the necessary lawyer fees. After getting divorced we continued living in the same household in a friendly manner for six months while planning for separate homes. Luckily I was able to locate a place for her to reside at one of my rental properties as a tenant at a discounted rate and this arrangement continues to this day, September 12, 2023. I was happy to do this because it provides a stable environment for my daughter, as well as benefitting my stepchildren whom I was able to help sponsor in facilitating their safe arrival to this country and acquiring all appropriate immigration documents. To this day I applaud their success and wish for their continual well-being.

I possessed a remarkable dedication to pursue both a full-time education and a full-time job as a park ranger for the city. Amidst the chaos of this dual endeavor, I unexpectedly encountered a lady who captivated my heart from the moment we met. She possessed an enchanting charm that effortlessly drew me in. Despite our genuine connection, I found it challenging to divert my attention from my demanding schedule to attend to this blossoming relationship. While I was wholeheartedly focused on my educational goals, this lady, who worked tirelessly as a nurse during the night, always found time to be there for us. She understood the demands of my work and studies, recognized the potential within me, and continued to be a source of encouragement and support. However, as time went on, this remarkable lady made the difficult decision to start anew in a small town in Alaska. Fueled by wanderlust and new opportunities, she embarked on the adventure of a different landscape and invited me to visit. Unfortunately, the weight of our commitments became an impediment for me to explore this opportunity and I couldn't accept her invitation.

This tangled tale serves as a testament to the unpredictable nature of life. Sometimes, despite genuine affection and shared connection, circumstances can conspire to separate individuals who hold a special place in each other's hearts. It reminds me that in certain situations, faith plays a significant role. Sometimes, it takes courage to let go and trust in the unknown. As I continued to work diligently towards my degree and excel in my desired goals, my thoughts often drifted to the lady who had shown me unwavering love and support. I sometimes wondered what might have happened if our paths had aligned differently. Life is a series of unique journeys intertwined with missed opportunities and unforeseen consequences. We can learn from experiences that while prioritizing our goals is important, it's also essential to treasure the connections and relationships that breathe life into our daily existence.

An interesting incident that involved a well-known athlete, Ray Lewis of the Baltimore Ravens, occurred at Patterson Park. Mr. Lewis was at a charity event in the park which caused extensive illegal car parking all over the vicinity. I had the authority to issue tickets and was required to enforce all park regulations, but I decided to just announce to them to move their cars, as the announcement was broadcast throughout the area, and most complied with the instructions. Somebody was bragging about his familiarity with Ray Lewis, so I decided to pretend not to know about his fame. The man said "You don't know who he is?", quickly becoming agitated. I further quipped "Nope, he's not a soccer player, right?" I warned him to immediately move his car or he would be cited with a $500 ticket, to which he angrily acceded to.

One thing that happened which I'm not proud of but nevertheless contributed to a good outcome, involved a young thug who tried to violate my personal space. As my partner, Doctor Jake, and I were bicycling through

Patterson Park a group of delinquent preteens approached us and at first seemed to be interested in us by asking questions such as, "Are you guys police" and "What do you guys do?" We interacted with them but continued to ride at a slow pace, with my partner ahead of me several yards. Then the gang surrounded me and continued peppering me with questions and all of a sudden one of the more unruly ones snatched the work phone from my belt. As soon as he attempted this I caught him by the collar, picked him up, and threw him roughly to the ground, twisting his arm, causing him to scream in pain and shame. They must have been part of the baseball group at the park because the coach came running towards them and grabbed another boy in an effort to quell the disturbance. Thus being resolved, we circumnavigated the park and witnessed a pitiful yet oddly satisfying site of the naughty boy hiding behind a tree when he saw us approaching. His playmates were mocking him and alerting us to his presence by pointing at him and laughing. One of the boys yelled that I almost broke his hand, but I secretly knew that I didn't because I could have very easily.

It was during my seventh year that I was assigned back to two different parks on opposite sides of the city, Druid Hill and Patterson Parks patrolling the areas with other rangers, especially some Spanish-born ones. We were appointed as special enforcement officers after training with the police department. There is an amusing anecdote related to my love of soccer and occurring after work. I didn't really know the intricacies of the game and would just kick high into the air, as was my instinct honed through Tae Kwan Do. My Hispanic friends would call me Ninja. I would frequently play pickup games with players already in the park and eventually would coordinate the Patterson Park Ranger team. Later I formed a team called Tango Bhutan and competed in various city leagues, winning many trophies until I joined my current team Chupa Cabras. We respect each other and even as we grow older continue to enjoy our times together.

While we patrolled the park as park rangers, we encoun-tered various situations, both good and bad. One incident that stood out and happened during the Stone Soul Picnic in Druid Hill Park, which was the largest gathering we had ever seen, with nearly a million people in attendance occurred as we were walking through the park, and we came across a pull-up competition set up by the United States Marine Corps (USMC). A man in the crowd spotted us and yelled, "I bet that park ranger can do this!" My coworkers encouraged me to give it a try, but I decided to play coy and pretended I didn't know how to do pull-ups. Intrigued, I made my way over to the stand and asked the organizers how it was done. However, they were skeptical of my intentions, as they believed my physique indicated that I could easily win.

The highest recorded count for pull-ups was 31, with the average rate of only 25 at that point. With subdued yet steady confidence, I agreed to participate. Carrying almost eight pounds of equipment, including a walkie-talkie, ticketing book, and two phones, I was advised to remove them, but I insisted on keeping them on. With the help of a participant, I jokingly retorted that the bar was too high and I needed help to reach it. I could have jumped to the bar but the heavy equipment prevented me from making that initial step. With all kidding aside and bravado and excitement to prove my gymnastic capabilities, I began the pull-up set. To everyone's surprise, I effortlessly completed 51 pull-ups, breaking the record. The crowd erupted in applause, and I was awarded the prize - a complete set of USMC shorts, hats, and shirts. My park ranger coworkers were incredibly proud of me and showered me with praise. Back at the station, all they could talk about was how I defeated the entire round of competitors which contributed to the uplifted morale of the entire park ranger team.

Another incident showcased a different side of me - a more authoritative one. My partner, Liz, and I were patrolling various parks in the city when we came across a man dumping his trash in Clifton Park. We approached him politely and informed him that he wasn't permitted to dispose of trash there. In response, he became aggressive, attempting to intimidate us. Feeling the need to stand our ground, I boldly told him that he shouldn't think he could scare us away. A heated argument ensued, and he threatened to report us to the park office. True to his word, he followed through with the complaint. When we returned to the office, our director called us in to discuss the incident. He was already aware of the situation but wanted to hear our side of the story. The man reported that I had attempted to use Kung Fu on him, a claim that was far from the truth. I explained I would have defended myself if he had physically attacked us, but our director understood the reality of the situation. He and my coworkers knew me as a gentle and caring person, and he also recognized that I could be tough and react accordingly when faced with adversity.

These incidents highlighted the dynamic nature of our job as park rangers. We encountered moments of triumph and moments that required us to assert our authority to maintain order. Through it all, we strove to protect our parks and ensure that everyone could enjoy the amenities in a safe and comfortable environment.

Chapter 9: BSN Program

After graduating from community college with a degree in general studies, the next step was focusing on nursing prerequisites for my Bachelor's in the health care field. This transition showed my commitment to building a strong foundation for my education and career. My interest in science led me to explore the University of Maryland Bio Park, where I took a few additional science classes and discovered my propensity for anatomy and physiology, the course I was most enamored of. This clearly showed a strong alignment between my passion for physical fitness and my desire to understand the human body's structure and functionality.

The college which I would be associated with, Sojourner Douglas, was near BCCC and closely related in a variety of ways. Meeting its president, Dr. Simmons was a stroke of luck, because he would frequently dine at the restaurant which my parents and I attended often. He offered encouragement and belief in me which motivated me to apply to his college. I was accepted with the transferred credits from my community college and opted to pursue a Bachelor of Science in Nursing (BSN) degree to further solidify my commitment and participation in the chosen field of study.

However, one major challenge I faced was the math requirement. Math had always been a struggle for me since

I did not have any foundation growing up, but thanks to my dear grandpa's tutoring, I was able to overcome it at community college. His experience in statistics and dedication to helping me succeed made a significant difference. Even though the advanced math classes in my BSN program were challenging, we persevered. While struggling to keep up in class, I made the most of my time at home by practicing with my grandpa. His early morning tutoring sessions, although filled with occasional arguments, proved to be invaluable, and our bond grew stronger through the process.

Completing the additional prerequisites and qualifying to apply for the BSN program was a significant milestone however, the entrance posed another hurdle, especially the math portion. Unfortunately, I did not pass the first time, but instead of losing hope, I dedicated the following six months to rigorous math practice. My determination paid off, and when I retook the test, I passed with flying colors. A week later, I received the acceptance letter into the BSN program. It was a moment of triumph and joy, and it marked the beginning of my journey toward becoming a registered nurse. I was enrolled in the BSN program and worked as a nursing support tech at Mercy Hospital to earn extra money and gain more "hands-on" experience.

Additionally, I had the opportunity to engage in a practicum at Northwest Hospital for two semesters. During my practicum at Northwest Hospital, my skills were put to the test. On my first day as a nursing student, I was assigned to care for two patients. One of them required assistance with cleaning his bedpan, which initially made me feel queasy. However, my supervisor was patient and supportive, making light of the situation and completing the task herself. Over time, I became more comfortable and accustomed to these duties, realizing that it was simply a part of the job. One incident arose which was quite funny. Clad in my white outfit with a stethoscope hanging from my neck many people mistook me for a doctor clearly surprised when I corrected them. Although this happened many times with the usual comment "You look like a doctor" accompanying their many startled reactions, these comments always surprised me. Since all of the students wore the same uniforms, I couldn't understand the mistaken appraisals.

Driven by my Buddhist belief in helping others and my natural inclination towards sympathy, I excelled in my job. I approached my work at the hospital with the utmost respect and empathy, particularly towards patients who were extremely ill and had no family members to assist them. Keeping my parents in mind, I felt a deep connection with those who were abandoned and helpless. My dedication to helping the most vulnerable patients earned me recognition from both management and coworkers. I often received praise and appreciation for my exceptional efforts in assisting the sick. Despite the challenges of working with people, my deep-seated love for the downtrodden kept me going. In my role at Mercy, I frequently encountered difficult patients, especially homeless individuals. While others were hesitant to deal with them due to their antagonistic behavior, I approached them differently. I took the time to build relationships, offering not only physical assistance but also emotional support. I learned their stories, helped them stay clean, and even offered them baths. One patient which I wasn't actually assigned to, was in a semi-comatose stage and was sort of unattended by the rest of the hospital employees. Even though I wasn't assigned to her, I felt pity for her and helped her with her particular care routine. She grew to recognize my presence whenever I was near her and smiled. No one had to ask me to do these tasks, it was forged as part of my earlier training as a monk to respect all sentient beings. Some coworkers were without much formal education/training and I recognized their lack of understanding in dealing with complex situations, which strained my patience, but ultimately I learned to deal with this factor of life. I must admit though that the laziest fellow workers created most of the tension in our interpersonal interactions.

My coworkers recognized my unique ability to handle difficult situations and rewarded me with accolades, including the prestigious employee of the year. However, as I progressed through my BSN program and continued my work at the hospital, I began to question whether nursing was truly the right path for me. Dealing with difficult patients and their entitled family members took its toll on me. I couldn't imagine myself doing the same job repeatedly and facing the constant challenges posed by unpleasant individuals.

After much contemplation, I decided to switch my program to healthcare administration. I discussed my concern with my advisor, who supported my decision and dedicated myself to intense studies, immersing myself in the world of healthcare administration. Eventually, the day came when I graduated with my degree in healthcare administration. While my path had taken a detour, I knew deep down that I made the right decision. My experiences as a nursing support tech have provided me with invaluable insights into the healthcare industry, and I was determined to make a difference in another capacity. As I embarked on my new journey, I held onto the lessons I had learned from my time as a nurse. My compassion, empathy, and ability to handle difficult situations would continue to guide me as I worked tirelessly to improve healthcare systems and ensure that everyone receives the care and support they deserve. And so my story serves as a reminder that our paths may change, but our core values and desire to help others remain constant. Sometimes, it takes a detour to discover the right path, and my journey was a testament to the power of self-reflection and the pursuit of one's true calling.

Chapter 10: MJ Morgan

A company that served as an incubator for many of my employment skills is MJ Morgan, where I learned valuable skills in employment management administration. My mentors and colleagues guided me, nurtured my potential, and encouraged me to take on new challenges. As an operations manager, I was responsible for overseeing the smooth functioning of multiple offices and ensuring the highest level of customer satisfaction.

Despite the demanding nature of my job, I found joy and fulfillment in my work. The company's culture of support and collaboration made each day enjoyable. I forged strong relationships with my assistants, who quickly became close friends. Together, we tackled obstacles, celebrated successes, and constantly strived to improve our services. As the years went by, my hard work and dedication did not go unnoticed. Thanks to the guidance and mentorship provided by my bosses, I received several promotions throughout my tenure. With each new role, I gained more responsibility and had the opportunity to make a great impact on the company and its clients. Not only did MJ Morgan invest in my professional development, but they also supported me personally. The flexibility they offered allowed me to balance my dual roles in management and recruitment within the company. This work-life balance enabled me to pursue additional opportunities and expand my knowledge in employment administration. Looking back, I am incredibly grateful for the chance encounters with their CEO, Michael J. Morgan, and Vice President Patrick Cosgrove at the gym which led to my employment at MJ Morgan. The company not only provided me with a platform to grow professionally, but it also became a second family. The bonds I formed with my colleagues were priceless, and they continue to be an integral part of my life.

As I reflect on my journey, I realize that while my job title may have changed over the years, my passion for employment management has remained steadfast. With the experience and expertise gained at MJ Morgan, I continued to make a positive impact in the employment recruitment industry, knowing that I had the support of an amazing team behind me.

The year was 2019 and my group of friends from the neighborhood decided to go on a camping trip in the beautiful wilderness of West Virginia. It was a gathering of three friends from Pennsylvania and three from Baltimore, and we were all excited for the adventure that awaited us. Each person packed plenty of food and drinks for the trip, ensuring that we had everything we needed to have a great time. Among the provisions and because I had not cooked on a fire in over 20 years since my time in Bhutan, I had packed two cases of wine and was prepared to demonstrate my culinary skills.

When we arrived at the campsite, our eyes were instantly drawn to the breathtaking surroundings. The place was filled with natural beauty, offering excitement and wonder at every turn. Our enthusiasm was contagious, and we wasted no time in getting settled and preparing for a memorable camping experience.

I was fueled by nostalgia and a desire to showcase Bhutanese culture and took charge of the fire-building duties. I led the group in collecting firewood, and anticipation built with each log we added to our growing pile. However, as our excitement grew, I ended up collecting far more firewood than we actually needed for the entire stay. Undeterred by my surplus of firewood, I stepped up to the task of cooking an authentic Bhutanese dinner for everyone to enjoy. With mouth-watering organic chicken curry and veggie curry on the menu, the aroma of the tempting victuals filled the campsite, making everyone's stomachs growl with anticipation.

As night fell, the weather was perfect for gathering around the bonfire. I was brimming with enthusiasm, eagerly demonstrating the Bhutanese method of creating a bonfire by igniting the large pile of firewood and proudly showcasing my skills to my friends. However, what we didn't realize was that there were rules in place regarding the size and location of the fire. The fire we had built, inspired by early childhood Bhutanese experience, quickly grew out of control, causing concern for the safety of the surrounding campsite. Park rangers had to be called in to intervene and extinguish the fire, bringing an end to my impromptu bonfire extravaganza. In the aftermath, as we tried to explain our actions to the park rangers, I humorously insisted that this was simply how we Bhutanese people camp and make fires. The story of my ambitious bonfire attempt was a favorite among the group, and it was retold countless times when we returned home, eliciting laughter and fond memories of our time in West Virginia. Despite the unexpected fire incident, the camp trip was an overall success. We friends had enjoyed the beauty of nature, the delicious Bhutanese dinner, and the warmth of our bonfire, even if it had been a bit larger than anticipated. It will forever be remembered as a wonderful time filled with shared laughter and unforgettable experiences.

Chapter 11: Randstad

As the final chapter of the excursion into my life story unfolds, I find myself filled with gratitude and a sense of fulfillment. My association with Randstad U.S.A., an international agency specializing in recruitment and professional human resource management, has been nothing short of incredible. I have the privilege and responsibility of overseeing a remarkable team of associates while tending to the needs of my clients.

Being part of an international agency specializing in recruitment and professional human resource management has been truly remarkable. What makes it even more exceptional is the fact that our location in Arundel County is just a short ten-minute jaunt from my home. This convenience allows me to oversee a remarkable team of associates and manage over one hundred and eighty employees who diligently tend to the needs of our valuable clients.

The swiftness with which I was promoted within this organization is a testament to my dedication and resourcefulness. Every day, as the sun rises, I find myself eagerly looking forward to my job. Having a rewarding and interesting position like mine is an absolute blessing. It instills a strong sense of purpose and excitement, as I am constantly motivated to tackle the challenges that lie ahead while guiding my assistants toward success.

One of the key factors that contribute to my enjoyment of work is the incredible people I have the privilege of working with. From my immediate assistants and friendly partners to my inspirational boss whose office is based in Pennsylvania, everyone plays a significant role in fostering a positive and supportive work environment. I am grateful for their constant support and collaboration, as it greatly contributes to my personal growth and the overall success of our team.

With each passing day, I eagerly anticipate many more years with this company. I am determined to persevere and embrace new challenges, as I aspire to make a positive impact in my field. My passion for work, coupled with the unwavering support I receive from my team, promises even greater opportunities for growth and advancement in the future.

Although these accomplishments are noteworthy, if I may be permitted to mention, I am still filled with humility, as coming from a humble background and fulfilling my childhood dream of succeeding in America has uniquely prepared me for that future.

While some people dread Mondays and the thought of going to work, I find myself eagerly looking forward to my job. Having a rewarding and interesting position like mine is truly a blessing. I wake up each day with a sense of purpose and excitement, eager to tackle the challenges that lie ahead. One of the key factors that make my job so enjoyable is the people I work with. My boss is not just a manager but a great leader who inspires and supports me. My colleagues are respectful and always eager to lend a helping hand. The positive and supportive work environment contributes to my and everybody else's growth and success.

With each passing day, I look forward to many more years with this company. I am determined to persevere and take on new challenges, thus making a positive impact in my field. My passion for work and the support I receive from my team ensure that the future holds even greater opportunities for growth and advancement. As I reflect on my journey, I realize how fortunate I am to have found a career that brings me joy, fulfillment, and a sense of purpose.

Chapter 12: Daily Routines

In addition to my dedication to work, family, and fitness, I have always believed in the importance of maintaining strong relationships with friends. Throughout my life in Baltimore, my daily routine has always revolved around these principles.

Every morning, my parents and I start our day by visiting the local coffee shop Koba Cafe. When they were employed with the federal government they would commute to work, sign in, and then return to join me at coffee at Sorso Café. It was a delightful spot owned by our cherished friend. With my education and employment now completed, the responsibility for the morning routine is reciprocated and I have taken on the role of facilitator. We usually sit there together for a while, sipping our drinks and enjoying each other's company. From there, I head off to the office, while my parents either remain at the coffee shop or walk back home. Although the coffee shop is just a block away, we usually drive there due to my need to quickly get to work. On the weekends, the routine slightly changes. Instead of driving, we prefer to walk to the coffee shop with my daughter allowing us to enjoy the fresh air and engage in a little exercise. We happily have breakfast together before strolling back home, cherishing these moments of togetherness.

One thing I never compromise on is our coffee time in the mornings and evening dinners together with my parents. My philosophy is to enjoy life while you can and while your loved ones are alive treat them well but don't regret when they're gone. No matter how busy life gets, I always make sure to spend quality time with my parents, indulging in conversation and savoring the simple pleasure of having a cup of coffee together.

On the weekends Saturdays are spent with my daughter focusing on activities in which she participates with her friends and classmates, concentrating on the game of soccer and other physical activities. Sundays are devoted to my favorite pastime, soccer, which has always fascinated me and has kept me physically fit, a good source of cardio workout. My reputation precedes me throughout the Baltimore soccer community, as my fellow athletes eagerly await whatever new moves I may bring to our friendly and spirited tournaments. At least four or five rambunctious games are played every Sunday, with many of the players from several different teams congregating at various city venues but usually at Patterson Park. I may not be the most skilled player, but as a striker, I compensate for any deficiencies by being tenacious as a bulldog and fast as a rabbit, resulting in the opposing defenders suffering from bouts of breathlessness chasing me all over the field. My personality does not allow other players to take advantage of me, but if instigated I will show no mercy and can become as aggressive or vicious as any other player on the field, while never resorting to unsportsmanlike behavior. If I try to outdo myself by dribbling, all bets are off because my skills aren't quite as honed as others who are more accustomed to the fine sport of soccer due to the fact that I was actually not allowed to squander my valuable time on extraneous activities while being trained earlier in life as a monk. Although these evening games occur on weekdays, I always make time to cater to my family.

After work, my focus shifts to a fitness routine. I make it a priority to hit the gym, not only to maintain my physical health but also to take care of my mental well-being. Exercise allows me to clear my mind and recharge for the rest of the evening as well and I get to interact with friends who possess the same interests and goals. Once I've completed my workout, I head home and begin my culinary adventures in the kitchen. Cooking for my family is a joyous activity for me. I take pride in preparing delicious meals that we can all enjoy around the dining table, and of course, a glass of wine to accompany the meals.

Every now and then, we like to treat ourselves by eating out at one of our favorite restaurants in the neighborhood - Tabrizi's. This charming establishment has become a regular spot for our group of friends as well. We love the convivial atmosphere and the opportunity to catch up with one another. It's truly a joy to spend time with our friends who share mutually our respect and kindness. What sets our group of friends apart is the genuine desire to support each other. Whether it's assisting in career advice or being there during challenging times in our personal lives, we can always count on one another. This network of trusted individuals creates an environment where everyone feels valued and cared for.

In essence, my life in Baltimore is a dynamic balance between dedication to work, spending quality time with my family, prioritizing my fitness, and cherishing the strong bonds of friendship. These routines have been the foundation of my lifestyle, allowing me to find fulfillment and happiness in all aspects of life.

Chapter 13: Romantic Pursuits

I must add that I have always possessed a deep love and appreciation for music, and throughout my life, I have found solace and joy in the art of composing beautiful melodies. Although I had put reading and writing Dzongkha scripture aside during 15 years of my study time here in America, it remains a part of me, deep in my soul. Just recently, I was reminiscing about my homeland and my love for music, and I felt a renewed desire to write songs once again. However, I hesitated since I had been away from my native language Dzongkha writing for so long, I feared I might have forgotten how to write and express myself properly.

Determined to overcome this obstacle, I decided to start immersing myself in the language again. In my spare time, I began reading and writing in Dzongkha. It was a struggle at first, as I had to reacquaint myself with what had once been known so well. Determination pushed me forward and in the year 2023, I regained my confidence to share my compositions with the Bhutanese film industry and completed seven compositions in a short period of time. I reached out to my good friends who are renowned artists such as Karma Phuntso, Lop Kinley Tshering, Phub Zam, Tenzin Wango, and Ugyen Seldon, offering them my heartfelt songs to perform. To my delight, the singers and popular musicians such as Karma Yonten, Tandin Dorji, and Jigme Wangchuk (of Lojig Studio) loved my compositions. One by one, they brought my songs to life, pouring their emotions into my melodies. I felt immense pride and gratitude as I heard my words being sung by these talented artists, who were greatly admired in the Bhutanese media.

Now that I have found success in the Bhutanese film industry, I also gained confidence in my ability to express myself in English. Encouraged by my highly educated friends, I began writing in English on social media platforms, utilizing Facebook and WeChat Telegram, to hone my interdisciplinary skills, and resulting in essays and seminal books. Some of these essays concerned such classics as love for my parents, friendship, and respect for our cultural heritage. I used my words to convey my thoughts, feelings, and experiences, thus attracting a growing audience who reacted to my heartfelt expressions. My journey taught me the power of perseverance and the importance of embracing one's passions, no matter how long they have been dormant. I understood that life would always present obstacles, but it was through determination and willingness to confront those challenges that one could rediscover their true calling. And so, I continued my musical journey, writing songs that touched the hearts of many, including a dedicated paean of love to my 85-year-old mom. This is a reminder to everyone that it is never too late to follow one's dreams.

As a coda to this story, we find ourselves in the year 2022, and I found myself in a unique situation. Not too long following my divorce, after 12 years of marriage, I decided to seize the opportunity to recreate my bachelor days. I signed up for various dating sites, eager to explore what modern dating had to offer. To my surprise, I started getting answered by a diverse array of women. It was a pleasant shock since I had never thought many women would be attracted to me at this stage of my life. I questioned myself, wondering if it was my charisma that drew them in, but I quickly dismissed that notion. It couldn't have been my looks either - it was something else entirely. Curiosity got the better of me, and I delved deeper into the dating scene.

I decided to approach each encounter with an open mind, trying to develop long-lasting connections. I initiated video calls with women, seeking to familiarize myself and make them comfortable before meeting face to face. I believed that a foundation built on friendship and a genuine connection would lead to stronger relationships. As the months went by, I found myself going on sixteen different dates. Each encounter held its own uniqueness, but I never truly connected emotionally with anyone, except for one special woman. She possessed everything I had been looking for - a kind heart, a beautiful soul, and shared interests that sparked a fire within me. Realizing that this woman was the one destined to be a significant part of my life, I made a decision to disable all my dating apps. I wanted to focus solely on pursuing a future filled with love and happiness together. To celebrate our love and express my feelings, I decided to write a song dedicated to my beautiful girlfriend Lhasey Yiwong. Little did I know that this song would catch the attention of the Bhutanese media and become a popular hit. The public could feel the genuine love and emotions expressed through the lyrics and melody. And so my temporary bachelor time turned into a transformative journey that led me to a love that was worth waiting for.

Chapter 14: Final Thoughts

I had always dreamt of having my own teachers and friends from Bhutan visit me in America. Little did I know that my dream was about to come true, validating my gratitude and pride for the aid that others provided.

As the years went by, I worked hard and created a life for myself in America. I have not only excelled professionally but also became well-connected in various social and business circles. My achievements caught the attention of influential figures, including dignitaries such as the Bhutanese finance and foreign ministers, the Speaker of the House, judges, and King Jigme Khesar Namgyel Wangchuck's assistants. One day an opportunity arose for me to extend an invitation to my beloved teachers and friends from Bhutan while they were visiting New York to perform a ceremony for Bhutanese living in North America. My ex-teacher, the former Tsugla Lopen Rinpoche Samten Dorji, was the first to visit. The reunion was joyous and filled with heartfelt conversations about past, and present circumstances, and future opportunities. My gratitude for the knowledge and guidance provided by Lopen Samten Dorji is immeasurable.

It was particularly gratifying to host both Bhutan's Minister of Foreign Affairs and Finance Ministers while they were visiting this country and conducting important affairs for Bhutan. Both were warmly welcomed to my house, as they arrived with their requisite entourage of assistants and other honorable cabinet members. They enjoyed learning about Baltimore and receiving a well-deserved respite from their hectic schedules. They even had the opportunity to visit our local casino and relax to the gentle pursuits of "a men's night out", while savoring all aspects of the activities which I provided for them. At the end of their visits I felt privileged to be treated as one of their equals, and to this day treasure the bonds which were forged. As a modern form of salutation, they even texted me when zooming by my adopted city of Baltimore, grateful to have been included at least for a moment, in another aspect of American life. They have indicated an eagerness to host me and my family when we return to Bhutan, and this to me is an example of life's greatest honors.

Additionally, the present Tsugla Lopen Rinpoche Khenchen Karma Rangdrol, another ex-teacher, accepted the invitation. I could hardly contain my excitement and happiness at having my esteemed teacher at my side once again. Rinpoche Khenchen Karma Rangdrol's teachings and wisdom had a profound influence on my growth, both spiritually and scholastically. He will always have a warm place in my heart due to his kind and extensive teachings. I composed a brief and heartfelt description of his life and influence on my spiritual development:

མགོན་པོ་ཁྱེད་གསུང་གངས་ཀྱི་རི་བོ་ལས། །

བབས་པའི་ལེགས་བཤད་བདུད་རྩིའི་ཐིགས་པ་འཐུམས། །

ཐོས་བསམ་སྒོམ་པའི་རྩོང་པ་བསལ་བའི་དུས། །

སྐྱར་ཡང་འཁྱུང་བའི་སྐལ་བཟང་འབྱུང་བར་སྨོན། །

His venerable Tsugla Lopen Rinpoche Khenchen Karma Rangdol is a renowned Buddhist monk who has made significant contributions to the religious community in Bhutan. He entered monkhood at a young age and completed all the necessary ritualistic processes required to enter a Shedra. He continued his studies at various Shedras, including Tango Buddhist University, where he excelled in

Buddhist philosophical studies and was among the first class of graduates.

During his time at Tango Lopen Rinpoche served as an assistant professor while still a student. His intellectual prowess and dedication to his studies earned him recognition, and after completing his studies and meditation practices, he was conferred the title of Khenpo. He was then appointed to serve at the Ngatsang Shedra (Buddhist Institute) in Mongar, becoming the first student from Tango University to receive this coveted appointment.

After moving to the eastern part of Bhutan, Lopen Rinpoche dedicated his time to establishing institutes of higher learning including Kanglung Buddhist College. His wisdom and knowledge were instrumental in promoting the monastic system and led to educational development in the region. His teachings flourished, as he prepared many highly qualified students throughout the country for advanced training and created opportunities for young people to pursue Buddhist studies and achieve spiritual enlightenment. As a result of his efforts, Buddhism has become more accessible to Bhutanese people from all walks of life, thus illuminating a path of spirituality and inner peace.

Lopen Rinpoche is a true exemplar of the principles of Buddhism: dedication, and discipline. His contributions to the Buddhist community in Bhutan have been invaluable and his teachings will continue to inspire future generations.

Tashi Delek

During Lopen Rinpoche's visit to perform a Zhbdrung Kuchoe anniversary of peri-nirvana in New York, he envisioned the establishment of a center called Pelden Drukpai Choetshog that would cater to the Bhutanese living in North America and serve as a means of preserving the rich cultural heritage of Bhutan. To turn this vision into reality, Lopen Rinpoche gathered a group of individuals who showed keen interest in helping establish the center. I am privileged to have been appointed one of the board members for this endeavor.

Allow me to introduce the seven board members: Ms. Snam Leki has been appointed as the President of the board, supported by Mr. Sonam Wangchuk as the Vice President and Treasurer. Additionally, we have five esteemed members: Ms. Tshokey Lhamo, Mr. Koencho Dorji, Mr. Tashi Yoezer, Mr. Pem Namgyal, and myself. Furthermore, we have requested Khenpo Nima Shar, a highly respected and esteemed individual to be the main person at the center. His presence will not only help guide and impart Buddhist teachings but also facilitate various religious activities for the benefit of the Bhutanese community during his stay in New York.

The reunion also included my dear friend Khenpo Nima Sha, who made the strenuous journey to America to improve his worldly knowledge. Khenpo Nima Sha also had a pivotal role during my time at Tango Buddhist University and his presence in the United States evoked a deep sense of gratitude and nostalgia. Reminiscing about my past I automatically think of my friend and fellow spiritual explorer Khenpo Nima Shar, who is also pursuing a worldly education to supplement his monastery teachings. I am so impressed with his knowledge and humility, that I wrote a brief biography outlining his fine qualities to social media. It is encapsulated below:

My friend Khenpo Nima Shar is a remarkable individual. He is a Buddhist scholar who is never satisfied with his level of knowledge and is always striving to learn more. Recently he has decided to come to America and pursue his English skills, which is a testament to his dedication to continual self-improvement.

From a young age, Khenpo Nima Shar exhibited an extraordinary desire to study classical Buddhist teachings and become a compassionate example of his Bhutanese culture. To this end, he joined the monk body at a young age and eventually entered Tango Buddhist University and studied higher Buddhist philosophical studies. He went through a rigorous process of instruction and deep ritualistic proceedings under the guidance of renowned teachers/Khenpos. Some of the Khenpos who ultimately reached the spiritual state of Nirvana are examples of revered ancestors and are well-known and affectionately respected.

Khenpo completed his Master's degree from Tango University and served as a lecturer for several years and then later entered three years of meditation immersion. He received Kagyue Wang Lung Thri Sum and many other teachings from His Holiness 68th Je Khenpo Tenzin Doendup and 70th Je Khenpo Trulku Jigme Choedra. Soon afterward he was conferred the title of Khenpo and served many years as principal of Sewla Shedra in Punakha. This path led him back to Tango University and he was well qualified to serve as Vice Principal. For a total of twenty years, he taught and conveyed knowledge to students pursuing higher studies.

All of this history of Khenpo's past prepared him for a prominent position in the teaching profession and the spiritual advisement of countless individuals that he lovingly prepared for time-honored traditions in the Buddhist realm. Honors include invitations to advise different sectors of the education system in Bhutan, and also teaching assignments in other countries, benefiting them tremendously. These countries included Japan, Singapore, Thailand, Taiwan, Hong Kong, Macau, Malaysia, Nepal and India. He is the author of several books and a researcher dealing with various levels of philosophy which continue to help people in all areas of government, religion, and education. This background of intense scholarship has earned him a place of honor among a large population of sincere followers of the Buddhist practice. At first, his renown was limited to written acclaim but now it has entered social media and governmental proclamations.

As an accomplished Buddhist scholar, Khenpo has dedicated his life to Buddha and sharing this pursuit with others. He has studied extensively and gained a deep understanding of Buddhist philosophy, theology, and practice. His knowledge is encyclopedic, and his ability to explain complex ideas in simple terms is impressive. Despite his considerable knowledge, Khenpo recognizes that there are gaps in his understanding particularly with regards to the English language. While he is fluent in Dzongkha and Tibetan and has a good command of other Asian languages, he recognizes that English is the language of international communication and diplomacy. Khenpo has taken a disciplined approach to improving his English skills and attends language classes regularly at the New York English Academy in Manhattan. He practices speaking with native English speakers and spends hours reading and writing in English. His commitment to learning is evident in his progress, as he has become more comfortable with the language and is able to convey his ideas clearly.

What is particularly inspiring about Khenpo's pursuit of English is that it exemplifies his spiritual value. As a Buddhist scholar, he believes that the pursuit of knowledge is an important aspect of the spiritual path. He sees learning as a means to expand his understanding of the world and to develop compassion for others. By persistently pursuing his English skills, Khenpo demonstrates the importance of self-improvement and the value of using knowledge to benefit all sentient beings. He acts in several roles to facilitate the happiness of followers and fellow Bhutanese in his adopted home of New York by teaching, advising, and demonstrating the asanas of yoga. A barometer of his dedication to others is that he is frequently on YouTube and other modes of communication. This dedication on his behalf encourages other serious devotees to tirelessly help others.

In conclusion, Khenpo is a truly remarkable individual. His dedication to learning and self-improvement is an inspiration to all who know him. His pursuit of English is a testament to his commitment to expand his understanding of the world and to better communicate with others. I am honored to call him my friend and look forward to seeing where his continual pursuit of knowledge takes him.

Throughout our time together here in Baltimore, my teachers, friends and I shared laughter, memories, and inspirational stories. The teachers were delighted to witness the success and dynamic life their former students had built in the United States. My achievements became a testament to the invaluable knowledge and guidance received from these remarkable individuals. By hosting my teachers and friends from Bhutan, we not only created cherished memories but this reunion also strengthened the bond between the two nations, America and Bhutan. It was a proud achievement to be able to bridge the gap, bringing a piece of Bhutan to America and showcasing the cultural exchange that had shaped my life. As the visit came to an end, I realized that this experience would forever hold a special place in my heart. It reminded me of my roots, the transformative power of education, and the importance of fostering connections that transcend geographic and cultural borders.

Reflecting on my journey, I understood that my most significant achievement was not only the ability to host dignitaries but also the fulfillment of a heartfelt dream. To share my success with teachers and friends from Bhutan was a testament to the enduring impact of their guidance and the strength of our friendship. From that point forward, I continued to honor my Bhutanese heritage while embracing the opportunities and experiences that America has to offer. I carried the teachings of my teachers with me, sharing our wisdom and inspiring others to chase their dreams while they remain eternally grateful for the invaluable role that teachers and friends from Bhutan had played in our remarkable journeys.

About The Author

Pema Tango is a former ordained Buddhist monk from Bhutan, having earned a Masters degree in Buddhist Philosophy from the major college Tango University. Traveling across India and ultimately America, he currently resides in Baltimore. He earned a Bachelor degree in healthcare administration from Sojourner Douglass College, and works for a major employment agency as a Senior Site Director. When he arrived in this country he spoke very little English, so is proud to present this book, a work of love, for many to enjoy.